The
Dream
Experience

The Dream Experience

Your complete dream workshop in a book

Brenda Mallon

A GODSFIELD BOOK
www.godsfield.co.uk

An Hachette UK Company
www.hachette.co.uk

First published in Great Britain in 2011 by
Godsfield, a division of Octopus Publishing Group Ltd
Endeavour House
189 Shaftesbury Avenue
London
WC2H 8JY
www.octopusbooksusa.com

Copyright © Octopus Publishing Group Ltd 2011
Text copyright © Brenda Mallon 2011

Distributed in the U.S. and Canada by Octopus Books USA:
c/o Hachette Book Group
237 Park Avenue
New York, NY 10017

ISBN 978-1-84181-400-1

A CIP catalogue record for this book is available from the British Library

Printed and bound in China

1 3 5 7 9 10 8 6 4 2

NOTE

A physician should be consulted in all matters relating to health and particularly in respect of pregnancy and
any symptoms that may require diagnosis or medical attention. While the advice and information in this book
is believed to be accurate, neither the author nor the publisher can accept any legal responsibility for any
injury sustained while following the exercises.

The meditation and visualization exercises included in this book are designed for relaxation and for
developing self-awareness. However, anyone who has emotional or mental problems, or who has had problems
of this nature in the past, should seek professional medical advice before attempting any of these exercises.
The author and the publisher accept no responsibility for any harm caused by or to anyone as a result of the
misuse of these exercises.

CONTENTS

CD tracks

TRACK 1: Music for Relaxation

TRACK 2: Meeting My Guide

TRACK 3: Re-Entering My Dreams

TRACK 4: My Creative Release

TRACK 5: My Healing Visualization

TRACK 6: My Astral Journey

TRACK 7: My Dream Wisdom

Introduction

Are you ready to explore the amazing world of your dreams? Are you ready to accept all the creative and spiritual insight they can offer you? I hope so, because this workshop in a book will guide you step by step through the many ways you can unlock the secret language of your dream world.

My book *The Dream Bible* describes more than 300 dream symbols and themes, which are universal across continents and cultures and have been with us for thousands of years. This book has grown out of that one – in order to show you how to work with your dreams, build your own dream archive and compile an intensely personal directory of dream symbols. It's like attending a workshop with me and sampling the tried and tested techniques I have used with thousands of people who, like you, wanted to explore their dreams. The reasons people come to workshops are many: to develop self-awareness, to get in touch with their intuition, or higher self, and to learn more about their spiritual path. As you work through the exercises, listen to the CD and chart the journeys taken by your dreaming self, you too will uncover new aspects of yourself and gain greater understanding of where you are now and where you need to go.

The journey begins

In my workshops and one-to-one dream therapy, I do not tell people what to think or what their dreams mean. The only person who knows the truth about your dreams is you, the dreamer. As in my practice, so in this book. I will act as your guide, companion and enabler, helping you to uncover the personal meaning of your dreams. I will carry a lantern that illuminates your dreams, sheds light on areas of darkness and allows you see more clearly. It's up to you to choose what you focus on and to decide the pace and direction of your journey as you discover more about your dreaming self. In each section of the book, you can decide when to move forward and when to take a break.

Throughout my life, dreams have played a significant role. They have guided me, alerted me to difficulties of an

emotional, physical and spiritual nature, and forewarned me of events. Sometimes they have been frightening, but unfailingly they have helped me. I know that dreams can have a huge emotional impact, so when using the book, take care of yourself and cherish your well-being. If a dream feels too emotionally charged or an exercise just doesn't feel right, then leave it and only return to explore it when you feel more grounded. It may be helpful to talk to a trusted friend if you are concerned about a dream; often practising the exercises with a friend or in a supportive group can be beneficial.

Dreamwork can bring you greater awareness of your intuitive self, offer solutions to all sorts of problems, indicate illness before you have overt symptoms and even help to heal difficult relationships. Working with your dreams also enhances creativity. Many of the creative-writing courses I run in Europe and the United States use dreams as the starting point for writing projects. In *The Dream Experience* you will find many examples of ways in which artists, writers, musicians and scientists have found the key to creativity through their dreams. I hope this journey will be the starting point of a fulfilling creative life for you, too. Wherever you are right now, with the dreams you are having right now, is the perfect place to begin this journey to uncover the inner wisdom contained in your dreams.

How to use the book and CD

This book has been designed to guide you through every stage of working with your dreams. It shows you how to record your dreams and build your personal dream directory and covers all aspects of dreamwork, from exploring dream characters and finding your dream guides to uncovering your powers of creativity and intuition. There are lots of suggestions to help you incubate, or bring about, dreams, plus activities to deepen your dreaming experience. In each chapter you are offered the choice to move on or to return to previous exercises, so that you work at your own pace and in a way that best suits you.

In the second part of each chapter you will find guided exercises and space on journal pages to record your dream experiences. Try to fill in the pages after completing each exercise. Then, later, you'll be able to look back at your entries and learn from the pattern and progression of your dreams. You may like to keep a dedicated dream diary alongside this, to help build your

personal dream archive. This will be particularly beneficial when you reach the final chapter of the book, where you learn ways to develop your dreamwork.

Using the CD

Listening to the music and guided instructions on the CD that accompanies this book will help you to reach a relaxed, contemplative state – the best state for focusing on dreams. The CD symbol at the bottom of a page tells you when to play the CD; just follow the simple instructions. There are musical interludes on the CD which give you time to explore a dream and use visualizations; you will be instructed when to return to the guided steps. Always work at a pace that suits you. If you need more time during an exercise, just pause the CD until you are ready to move on. If you prefer, you can follow the scripts at the back of the book (see pages 241–50) or record your own instructions. You might like to play the first track – just music – to help you to relax as you work through many of the exercises in the book.

Recording your experiences

Following each exercise you will find journal pages on which to record your thoughts and experiences. There are questions here, too, to direct your attention and focus your thinking, so you get the most from each exercise. When you write on the journal pages, use the first person ('I') and the present tense ('I can see', 'I am visiting') and write using an active voice ('I feel this' rather than 'This was felt'). These writing techniques give your writing a vibrant quality and lend immediacy. They also help to keep the exercise grounded in the here and now. Try to include as much detail as possible as you record your thoughts. Seemingly insignificant details often hold a kernel of truth that can easily be overlooked.

Write down your first thoughts, and try not to censor them or judge yourself. This is *your* personal record, and it is important to be true to yourself. Use all your senses as you record your dream experiences. Make a note of physical experiences in your body, thoughts that flit through your mind, sensations of touch and taste, and any images that arrive unannounced – all deepen your experience of the exercise. Sometimes you will have a sense of understanding after the exercise; do record such intuitive flashes, which offer information from your 'higher' self.

You may find that some time after completing an exercise you have further insight. Go back to the journal entries and fill in the fresh material, including the date. With dreams, you may only understand the message years after the experience, often because you were not ready to receive that message any earlier.

Throughout the book you will find images to help you visualize aspects of your dreamwork. For example, you might contemplate the images of dream 'power' animals and imagine how their characteristics might manifest in you: the speed of a cheetah, the agility of a mountain goat or the grace of a gazelle. Use them to help you build a unique personal archive of dream imagery. If you are not sure what some dream images mean, look them up in *The Dream Bible*.

The symbols in this book

Throughout the book you will find the following symbols, which will guide you as you journey into your dreams:

Work with this exercise now This symbol guides you to the correct page, tells you how to proceed with the exercise, and includes the appropriate CD track number, if applicable, and the page number on which you will find the script.

I'm not there yet If you feel unready to complete an exercise or unable to work on a certain dream or image, leave the exercise for now and return to it at a later date when you feel more grounded and emotionally robust. Always take the exercises at a pace that suits you. This symbol suggests other exercises to help open you to this particular form of dreamwork.

When to do this exercise This suggests a time of day or a situation in life when this form of dreamwork might be especially beneficial.

Work with the CD now This symbol tells you when you need to turn on the CD and which track to select. If you would like to follow the script to the CD, turn to the pages indicated.

Glossary of terms

Archetypes
Archetypes are inherited mental images or symbols occuring across cultures and throughout history.

Chakra
From Sanskrit 'wheel'. The chakra system locates rotating energy centres along the spine linking the physical body with its circulating subtle energy. When this energy is disturbed by emotional or physical distress, chakras become blocked. Dreams can indicate chakras needing attention.

Higher being/self
The wise part of you that transcends everyday consciousness to access spiritual realms and the divine; the best you are capable of being.

Individuation
An individual's search for greater self-understanding, personal integration and self-fulfilment.

Life force
Part of human anatomy or subtle body invisible to the eye; influences all activities and governs physical and emotional well-being.

Psyche
From Greek 'soul or mind'. This self encompasses all psychic processes including that which is conscious or known to us, and the unconscious.

Shadow
An archetype; that part of our nature we hide from others or ourselves. May appear in dreams as a dark, threatening figure.

Shaman
Person who can access the natural and supernatural worlds. Seeks out knowledge and power from spirits to bring healing and understanding to a community.

Subconscious/unconscious
Part of the mind below normal consciousness or awareness that influences our thoughts, actions and dreams. Followers of Sigmund Freud use the term 'unconscious mind'; followers of Carl Jung 'subconscious mind'.

Beginning your journey

With practice, you will learn how to focus on the meaning of your dreams, but it helps to feel calm and at peace before you start your dreamwork. So take time now, as you begin this wonderful journey, to relax your mind and body. This exercise shows you how to relax and gently make room for your dream world to enter your waking world.

Work with the CD now Lie down in a comfortable position in a warm room. Make sure you won't be disturbed, so you can become fully involved in the relaxation. Now play Track 1 of the CD. Close your eyes, listen to the relaxing music and let your worries go as the sounds wash over you. Focus on your inner self, the dreamer of dreams. When the music ends, open your eyes gently and roll over onto one side before sitting up slowly to maintain the sense of relaxation for as long as possible.

THE STORY OF DREAMING

What are dreams?

There are many definitions of the word 'dream'. One of the most commonly used describes dreaming as 'a mental activity usually in the form of an imagined series of events, occurring during certain phases of sleep' (*Collins English Dictionary*). Dreaming is the result of the brain being active while the body's sense organs and major muscle groups are switched off to external stimulation.

Sleep is a progression of cycles involving different phases of brain and body activity, repeated every 90–110 minutes. In Stage 1 sleep, muscles relax and the heart rate slows. Stage 2 is marked by 'spindles', quick bursts of brain activity, and Stage 3 sleep by large slow brainwaves. By Stage 4, delta sleep, we are deeply asleep. REM (Rapid Eye Movement) sleep happens in Stage 5, when dreaming takes place. In this condition, the mind creates experiences from our current preoccupations, memories and fantasies. It also works on our concerns of the day. As we sleep and dream the events of our waking life are stored and the neural systems involved in learning, memory, attention and emotional activities are renewed. When dreaming is prevented, long-term memory and data processing are disrupted.

Dreams are encoded messages from one part of the brain to another. While we are dreaming, the brain is most active in the limbic system, particularly the amygdala. It is in this part of the nervous system that emotions are processed and memories formed, using symbols to convey meaning rather than rational language. So in order to interpret the unique meaning of our dreams and

enhance our understanding of the connections between mind and body, we need to learn this symbolic language and use it during our waking hours.

Some people describe dreams as 'visions of the night', though they may be sensory rather than visual experiences since we know that blind people dream. The dreams of visually impaired people are based on the other four senses – touch, smell, taste and sound. One client told me he knew a dragon was in his dream because he could smell the smoke it breathed out and feel its scaly coat. We all have a sixth sense, too, that may be revealed in dreams – an intuitive or psychic sense. In chapter 6, for example, you will meet Maria, whose dream of an road accident forewarned her to slow down and avoid a real accident.

Benefits of dreamwork

This dream workshop in a book will show you how dreams can help you as a person in so many ways. As you work through the exercises, you may feel more in touch with your innate creativity, intuition and ability to heal. You will gain a deeper understanding of what motivates you, and find ways to lead a more fulfilling life, becoming the person you always wanted to be. Dreams also present you with an opportunity to try out things you would not experiment with in your waking life. On one level, they may offer compensation for aspects lacking from your everyday existence, perhaps to do with sex, travel or friendship. People who have had a limb amputated, for example, may dream that their body is whole once more.

Dreams can offer opportunities for development at a community and world level, too. The social dreaming movement meets in groups across the globe to share dreams and reflect on them. In doing so, participants find connections and establish links between individual dreams. If we do this, we might find that our dreams voice similar concerns – about threats to the environment, wildlife and the future of our communities – and in those shared dreams we might also find solutions to such global problems.

 Work with this exercise now Find a quiet place where you will not be disturbed, then turn to Exercise 1: The Story of My Dream on page 34 and follow the instructions.

Enhancing dream recall

If you practise good sleep hygiene, not only will your sleep be enhanced, you will be better able to recall your dreams. These are the sleep-hygiene essentials: try to go to bed at the same time each night, keep your bedroom free of distracting clutter such as computers and work-related papers, and use elements such as soft lighting, fresh bedlinen and a calming colour scheme to ensure that your room becomes a place of sensual retreat.

How and what we dream is highly dependent on what we do before we sleep. Sometimes the symbols and activities in our dreams reflect what's going on in our waking lives. Dreams seem to respond to positive energy, so when you are awake, try to respond positively to whatever life throws at you. Look for win-win outcomes and celebrate your successes, however minor they may be. Building up stores of positive energy during our waking hours

nurtures hidden potential and allows it to surface in dreams. So before you sleep, go back over your day in your mind and consciously clear out the 'debris' – people and situations that drain you of positivity or which you would rather not dwell on. By doing this you help your psyche to be more innovative and creative, which frees your dreaming self to experience more extraordinary dreams. You can develop this further by requesting a special dream just before you fall asleep.

Difficulties of remembering

Everyone dreams, but some people find remembering their dreams difficult. There are some good reasons why you might be struggling to remember your dreams. If stress and fatigue consume much of your energy in your waking hours, the energy required for remembering dreams may be depleted. Medication may reduce dreaming, too. Cultural or religious beliefs may inhibit some people from contemplating their dreams; in some traditions dreams are considered unholy. If you are affected by any of these factors, do think about how you can change to allow your dreaming self to flourish. There are a number of practical techniques you can add to the good sleep-hygiene essentials to enhance your dream recall.

Talk to yourself During the day, tell yourself that you are going to remember your dreams.

Visualize yourself dreaming Imagine yourself having a dream and then waking up to record it.

Try a little meditation A period of contemplation helps to release stress and develops your intuition.

Take more vitamin B Research suggests that vitamin B, particularly B6, helps to increase the vividness of dreams. It may be helpful to take a supplement (check with your doctor first).

Stop drinking Abstain from alcohol, which has been shown to interfere with dreaming sleep.

Don't move When you wake, lie still and try to capture whatever image or emotion comes to mind. However fragmentary the image or feeling, hold it in your mind and then write it down.

Record your impressions Write down what was on your mind before you woke if you can't remember the dream itself. Don't worry if it's only a vague, fleeting memory.

Ancient techniques

The ancient Chinese, Egyptian and Japanese peoples used ceramic and wooden head rests in bed, believing that comfortable pillows would reduce the body's vitality. To aid sleep and dreams, they filled compartments in the head rests with herbs and spices. Some of the ceramic rests were even filled with hot water, to warm the neck and head of the sleeper. Chinese children were sometimes given double-headed tiger pillows so the most propitious animal in the Chinese mythological world would guard against any demons of the night that might surface in their dreams.

Today, we might use herbs, essential oils or crystals to aid deep sleep and dream recall. To experiment with your own dream recall abilities, try sleeping with a lavender pillow or place a few drops of essential oil of lavender in a diffuser in your bedroom. Alternatively, substitute essential oil of rose, which aids meditation, visualization and dream recall.

Using a crystal

To use a crystal to aid dream-recall, choose one that appeals to you from the chart opposite. Place the crystal in your left hand for 20 minutes and keep your

right hand open, ready to receive energy. Ask the crystal, either out loud or silently, to help you dream about whatever matters most to you at this point in your life. Then ask your higher self to work with the crystal. Place the crystal beneath your pillow; before going to sleep repeat your request.

Before using a crystal to make a new dream request, cleanse it. Either place the crystal in a bowl of uncooked brown rice overnight, asking that it be purified. Next morning, rinse the crystal under running water, dry with a clean cloth and place in sunlight to complete the process. Alternatively, place the crystal in a net, set it in natural running water and leave for several hours, again asking that it be purified.

CRYSTALS TO PROMOTE DREAMING

Amethyst Promotes restful sleep and enhances the quality of dreams. A crown-chakra crystal, it connects you with a higher force, or divinity.

Ametrine Aids your ability to absorb inner wisdom from your dreams. Linked to the crown chakra.

Azurite Helps you to access your power of intuition and psychic abilities. Stimulates the third-eye chakra at the forehead.

Celestite Aids dream recall and spiritual development. Linked to the crown chakra.

Clear Quartz Helps to amplify your dreams, making them more vivid and easier to recall. Linked to all the chakras.

Lapis Lazuli Aids dream-recall. Linked to the throat chakra.

Lepidolite Calms anxiety and reduces nightmares. Contains the natural form of lithium, which is used as a medication to treat mental health disorders linked to acute anxiety. A crown-chakra crystal.

Moldavite Can change the quality of your dreamwork when used with other crystals of your choice, giving you even more insight into the wisdom hidden in your dreams. This is a crystal of transformation, linked to all the chakras.

Smoky Quartz Discourages nightmares. Linked to the root chakra at the base of the spine.

Dream charms, talismans and amulets

Around the world and for centuries, people have tried to create the most conducive atmosphere for sleep and dreaming by placing objects under the pillow and next to or above the bed. These have many functions, including protection, because many communities believe the soul travels during sleep. Charms are objects worn or carried for their power to protect, heal and attract fortune; talismans are natural objects used to bring fortune and power to the holder; and amulets are specially created to ward off negative energy and illness.

Some of the earliest dream charms were natural objects, such as stones, in which holes had formed. Known as 'hag stones' in Britain and Europe, they were named after the evil spirit in many traditions known as 'Hagge', who is synonymous with the night 'mare'. *Maere* was the Old English name for this demonic night rider, and hag stones kept her from 'riding' the sleeper and leaving her 'haggered' next morning. The stones were usually threaded on a piece of wool and hung above the sleeper's head.

In other traditions, unusually shaped or patterned pebbles, shells, pieces of driftwood or other found natural objects were valued for their protective powers. Sometimes protective emblems were carved into wooden bedposts. In the 19th century, American author Mark Twain brought back a bed from Venice on which were carved angels, which he believed brought 'peace to the sleepers and pleasant dreams'.

Amulets were made to protect the wearer from harm. In some countries they took the form of a god who would protect the dreamer as he slept. In ancient Egypt this was the dwarf god Bes. In later eras, protective symbols were borrowed from various spiritual traditions to serve the same purpose – a cross, images of the Madonna, Hindu gods or holy leaders – or sacred words might be used for protection, with prayers or religious texts inscribed

on paper or etched in glass. All these techniques are still in use today.

African sleep charms sometimes come in the form of beaded dolls dressed as healers, used to protect sleeping children from evil spirits. Native American dream catchers decorated with feathers are now employed throughout the world. The hole in the centre of the dream catcher allows good dreams to reach the dreamer while distressing dreams are trapped in the warp and weft of the outer weaving.

 Work with this exercise now Pick a natural object, charm or amulet, then turn to Exercise 2: Enhancing My Dreams on page 38 and follow the instructions.

Recording your dreams

When you start recording your dreams you will be amazed at the insights that arise, especially once you have compiled a dream-record history. This habit can change your life in dramatic ways, as you will find when you work through the exercises in this book.

Recording your dreams gives you an ongoing archive that charts your personal development. It provides the information you need to spot connections with events in your waking life and understand how they are reflected in your dreams. As you record your dreams, you will start to see that the triggers for your dreams lie not only in your day-to-day life, but in past experiences and future hopes and plans. After keeping notes for a while, you will be able to see how far you have developed over a period of time. Your dream record may show, for example, how you have changed from being unable to express your feelings – perhaps in early dreams you are silent – to being able to say what you think and feel – in later dreams you may communicate clearly.

How to record your dreams

The best way to remember your dreams and build on the wisdom they bring is to keep a dream diary in parallel with the journal pages in this book. Keep the diary and a pen by your bedside so you can note down the details of a dream as soon as you wake up. The narrative of the dream will be clearer if you write it down immediately and try to make time during the day to analyse the dream while it is fresh in your mind. Freely make associations with the dream, connecting it with any relevant waking events. If you leave the dream analysis too long, you may forget such details.

Look for a dream diary with unlined pages – these make it easier to include drawings alongside your words. When you write in your diary, use the present tense and active voice (see page 12). Here is a good format for each dream:

Date and place Before going to sleep, write where you are sleeping and the date at the top of a new page. The location may influence your dreams. If you are staying in the house you grew up in, for

example, your old bedroom may trigger a dream related to your childhood. An impersonal hotel room may bring about quite different dreams. When we are away from our usual lives and routines, dreams may have more vivid imagery and you can remember them more easily.

Write it down On waking, write down the dream. Note form is fine – the important thing is to capture the essence of the dream – but if you have time, record the details. Include drawings or illustrations if this enhances your sense of the dream experience.

Dream title Once you have written down the dream, give it a title. Some titles jump out at you, some will feel inspired and others just reflect the basic content of the dream. Whatever works for you is fine – just try not to censor the first idea that comes into your head. Giving a title to your recorded dreams will help you remember them over a period of time, and we understand new dreams better in the light of older ones. When you take your dreamwork further (see pages 209–40), these titles will help you to analyse your unique pattern of dreaming.

First and final dreams If you have a rich dream life and recall many dreams from one night, try to record the dreams in order from first to last. In a series of dreams, the first dream often sets the scene while the final dream, just prior to waking, gives practical, problem-solving insight.

 Work with this exercise now Turn to Exercise 3: My Dream List on page 42 and follow the instructions.

Incubating dreams

Dreams have enormous potential to guide you and enhance your waking life. In order to maximize this potential, as well as learning to interpret a dream, you can use incubation techniques to bring about dreams that address problems or deepen your awareness of your true self. In dream incubation we call to our higher selves, God or the forces that shape our world. The technique helps bring about a dream that assists spiritual development, gives birth to new ideas or helps resolve simple, practical matters, such as finding lost objects.

In Ancient China, dream incubation was so respected that any high official visiting a city first reported to a temple to seek guidance from his dreams – seeking the wisdom and insight required for the mission at hand. Five thousand years ago ancient Greeks also practised dream incubation. At the peak of this dream-incubation culture more than 420 temples were dedicated to Asclepius, the god of healing. Healing temples were built and consecrated in his honour, the most famous being the Temple of Epidaurus. These temples were staffed by temple priests and priestesses who were part physician, part shaman, skilled in diagnosis, herbal cure and incantations, and with an extensive knowledge of dream interpretation.

The temple priests prepared a dreamer for sleep by carrying out cleansing rituals. Then the supplicant stated their request and slept in the sacred temple. Dream incubation without such preparation was unacceptable, ritual being central to the process. The aim was to stimulate a dream from an oracular or healing god.

On waking, the dreamer spoke of his or her dream and the temple priest offered an interpretation. The temple attendants not only interpreted the dreams of those who sought answers to problems and cures for illnesses, they prescribed medicine based on the nature of the dream. After this, the dreamer offered thanks and in some cases paid to have a stone or *stele* erected with a dedication, to indicate the part of the body healed and to venerate the power of the god.

We remain connected with this dream-aware world, not only in our dream investigations but through our language. The daughters of Asclepius – Panacea and Hygieia – gave us the words 'panacea' or cure-all and 'hygiene'. The sacred place to recline in the temple was called *kline*, which gave us the word 'clinic'. Those ancient dream-healing centres inform our current health systems.

Practical techniques

You, too, can invite dreams into your sleeping world – but not by bullying them or seeking to control them in a dominating way. Instead, let them be elusive and simply stay receptive to them using the techniques below. Dreams will come when you are ready to accept them. Welcome your dreams as you would a friend, even if they bring bad tidings. Love the messenger even though you may not love the content.

Request a dream Before you sleep, ask for a dream, holding the invitation lightly in your mind as you fall asleep.

Reflect on the dream When you wake, invite different aspects of the dream to reveal their message to you. Don't fret if the meaning is not clear; you may not be able to appreciate it yet. During the day, the dream may come into your mind or a specific event trigger a recall.

Write it down When you have time, jot down any meanings you understand in your dream diary, and record connections between specific events and your dream. Think about the dream setting, characters involved and any unusual aspects and include your thoughts about them in your diary.

 Work with this exercise now Turn to Exercise 4: Incubating My Dreams on page 46 and follow the instructions.

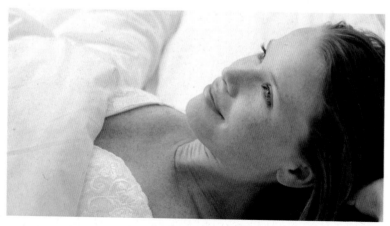

PREPARATORY
EXERCISES

These exercises will help you to understand your earliest dreams and deepen your awareness of the spiritual dimension of dreaming. They will show you how you can enhance your dreams through the inclusion of crystals, amulets and herbal preparations.

Writing my story

This writing exercise is a way of reflecting on your childhood dreams. They often contain the seeds of your early personality, and your abilities, fears and strengths. Thinking about them now can put your present dreams in perspective. You will need a notebook and pen.

Exercise 1 THE STORY OF MY DREAM
CD REFERENCE TRACK 1 (OPTIONAL)

When to do this exercise Try practising when you feel relaxed and can devote at least 20 minutes just to writing.

- **Choose a particularly vivid dream** or a nightmare you had when you were younger. Try to recall the 'plot' or storyline, and details about the characters and setting. Think about your age in the dream and where you were living.

- **Now write down the dream** as if you were writing a story. Make sure you flesh out the characters, describe the setting and include the whole storyline, beginning, middle and end.

- **When you have finished writing**, read over your story and give it an appropriate title. Now answer the questions on page 35.

My story of my dream experience

Questions to consider
How old was I when I first had this dream?
Where did I live when I had this dream?
What was my younger dream self saying to me?
How does this dream story reflect the life I was living then?
What major changes have happened in my life since then?

Date _____ Time _____

_____

_____

_____

_____

_____

Date _____ Time _____

_____

_____

_____

_____

_____

Date _____ Time _____

_____
_____
_____
_____
_____
_____
_____
_____
_____

Date _____ Time _____

_____
_____
_____
_____
_____
_____
_____
_____
_____
_____

Date _____ Time _____

_____

_____

_____

_____

_____

_____

_____

_____

Date _____ Time _____

_____

_____

_____

_____

_____

_____

_____

_____

Dream-enhancing

Many physical objects have been used over the centuries to enhance sleep and dreaming. This exercise allows you to explore objects you are naturally drawn to, which may bring you into deeper contact with your spiritual nature and so your dreams. You will need a number of objects to use as charms or amulets (see page 24–25), either man-made or natural.

Exercise 2 ENHANCING MY DREAMS
CD REFERENCE TRACK 1 (OPTIONAL)

∞ When to do this exercise This is best practised just before you go to bed.

- Over a period of a week, choose some objects that you feel will enhance your dream recall, perhaps a stone with a hole, a dream catcher or an attractive pebble.

- Place each object in turn close to your bed over the week. Look at and contemplate the object as you fall asleep.

- Next morning, record your dreams. If you don't remember your dreams, write down your impressions or the emotions you felt on waking. Then consider the questions on page 39 to help assess your reactions to each of the dream enhancers.

My dream-enhancing experience

Questions to consider
What drew me to each of my dream-enhancers?
What do they bring to my dream world?
How do I feel now about each of the dream enhancers I chose?

Date _____ Time _____

_____
_____
_____
_____
_____
_____
_____

Date _____ Time _____

_____
_____
_____
_____
_____
_____
_____

Date _____ Time _____

_____

_____

_____

_____

_____

_____

_____

_____

_____

_____

Date _____ Time _____

_____

_____

_____

_____

_____

_____

_____

_____

_____

_____

Date _____ Time _____

_____
_____
_____
_____
_____
_____
_____
_____

Date _____ Time _____

_____
_____
_____
_____
_____
_____
_____
_____

Listing my dreams

Sei Shonagan, born around 965, was an attendant of a Japanese Empress and compiled a *Pillow Book*, revealing her observations about life at court. It included her reminiscences, dreams and lists. One such list detailed 'things that should be short.' In this exercise, you make your own list to use as a prompt for your dreams. You will need a notebook and pen.

Exercise 3 MY DREAM LIST
CD REFERENCE TRACK 1 (OPTIONAL).

 When to do this exercise At the start of your dreamwork journey, to help you prioritize and commit yourself to your well-being.

- **Sit quietly and reflect on your dreams.** Are there events in your dreams that you would prefer to be shorter? If, for example, you were being chased and afraid, you could shorten the experience by imagining a friend coming to your rescue or by going to a safe place where you are known and protected. Make a list of the events you would shorten now.

- **Are there events in your dreams** that you would prefer to be longer. If, for example, you were enjoying a walk with a friend, you could imagine this extending into a longer journey that takes you into a different, glorious landscape. Make a list of the situations you would lengthen. To shed light on your thoughts, ask yourself the questions on page 43.

My dream list experience

Questions to consider

How did thinking about which dream events should be shorter affect me?
How did thinking about which dream events should be longer affect me?
How can these lists help me prioritize my time?
How can these lists help me prioritize my commitment to my well-being
and personal development?

Date _____ Time _____

_____

_____

_____

_____

_____

Date _____ Time _____

_____

_____

_____

_____

_____

Date _____ Time _____

_____

_____

_____

_____

_____

_____

_____

_____

_____

Date _____ Time _____

_____

_____

_____

_____

_____

_____

_____

_____

_____

Date _____ Time _____

_____

_____

_____

_____

_____

_____

_____

_____

_____

Date _____ Time _____

_____

_____

_____

_____

_____

_____

_____

_____

_____

Using the DARES method

I have devised this simple method to help you incubate the dreams you desire: DARES stands for Decide on an issue, Ask a question, Repeat it, Expect a dream, then Sleep. The process is straightforward to follow.

 ## Exercise 4 INCUBATING MY DREAMS
CD REFERENCE TRACK 1 (OPTIONAL).

 **When to do this exercise** Practise before you go to bed and sit quietly as you do the exercise.

- **Decide on the issue** you would like to consider in your dreams. You may want to understand why a relationship is going through a rocky period, perhaps, or be searching for ways to improve your interview skills.

- **Try to formulate your request as a question,** such as 'What is happening in my relationship at the moment to make it so rocky?' or 'How can I improve my performance at my next interview?'

- **Now ask the question,** either out loud or silently. Be as clear as possible and phrase the words in a positive way.

- **Repeat the question.** This helps to fix the intention firmly in your mind. Then expect your dreaming self to respond to your question, and get on with your everyday life.

- **When you are ready for bed,** go to sleep maintaining your expectation of a positive result.

- **On waking,** record your dream on the following pages as soon as possible, using the questions on page 47 to prompt your responses.

My dream incubation experience

Questions to consider
What effect did the dream incubation have on my dreams last night?
How did my dreams answer my question?
What can I change in my waking life as a response to the message in my dreams?

Date _____ Time _____

_____

_____

_____

_____

_____

_____

Date _____ Time _____

_____

_____

_____

_____

_____

_____

Date _____ Time _____

_____

_____

_____

_____

_____

_____

_____

_____

_____

Date _____ Time _____

_____

_____

_____

_____

_____

_____

_____

_____

_____

_____

INTERPRETING YOUR DREAMS

Dream interpretation

There have been professional interpreters of dreams for thousands of years. The ancient peoples of Babylon, Judea and Chaldea recognized dream interpretation as an accomplished art. As with later cultures, they regarded dreams both as omens and a means of communication between mankind and the divine.

Morpheus, the Greek god of dreams, gave his name to the *Oneirocritica* or *The Interpretation of Dreams*, one of the first books written and only the second to be printed on the Gutenburg press. Comprising five volumes written by Artemidorus of Daldis, Asia Minor, in the second century CE, this is the first comprehensive work on dream interpretation, and dominated the field until 1899, when the father of psychoanalysis, Sigmund Freud, published his major work under the same title. Freud's work had a huge impact on the way we understand the power of the unconscious mind.

The Epic of Gilgamesh, probably the oldest story on earth, dating from at least 2,000 CE, was written on twelve clay tablets and contains the first recorded sequences of dreams from different dreamers. In this story of the quest for immortality, the hero Gilgamesh reports to his goddess mother Ninsun dreams that foretell terror and tragedy. In one dream Enkidu, the travelling companion of Gilgamesh, sees the afterlife, and thereafter the certainty of life after death influences his world view and actions. The story of Gilgamesh is the first recorded example of dream incubation and dream interpretation as a form of guidance.

A spiritual tradition

Dream interpretation has played a part in all major religions. The primary texts of Hinduism, the *Vedas*, the earliest of which was composed around 1,500 CE, contain a section devoted to dreams. The famed interpreter of dreams Mohammad Ibn Sirin, born in modern-day Iraq in the eighth century, wrote the Islamic dictionary of dreams, *Dreams and Interpretations*, as a means of analysing past and future situations. In Japan, an official group of dream interpreters called *on myoshi* evolved, and those who

were ill would sleep in sanctuaries devoted to the bodhisattva Yakushi, hoping he would appear as a monk in their dreams and offer healing. In the Chinese tradition, dream analysis is thought to offer insight into an individual's inner life and help bring about positive change. Zhou Gong's *Book of Auspicious and Inauspicious Dreams* offers interpretations of all types of dreams, including dreams about spirits, music, home, the planets and all living creatures.

A new language

Interpreting dreams can be a challenge because the language of dreams is one of symbols, metaphors and archetypes, which may not always make its meanings transparent. By learning this hidden language, we gain access to the many layers of the dreaming world and discover the inner forces that push us into so many things, from relationships to jobs. We are often unaware of these hidden influences. Transactional Analysis, which looks at the psychology of human relationships, names them 'drivers', because they steer our behaviour and decision-making as adults.

Problem-solving

The old adage 'sleep on it' recognizes that the sleeping mind continues to aid the waking state. In our dreams we sift through daily experiences, sort out waking concerns and find solutions to ongoing problems. This is demonstrated in the work of Dr Rosalind Cartwright of Rush University Medical Centre, Chicago, whose research studied the dreams of recently divorced women. The women spent a great deal of time in dream sleep (see page 18); in fact, Professor Cartwright discovered that they were dreaming in the same way as young babies do when sorting out the massive amount of sensory information in the developing brain. It appeared that the women needed to carry out 'emotional reprogramming' as they adjusted to their new situation.

Dreams often provide clues as to how we are coping with problems. They draw attention to an issue over and over – until we consider it during our waking hours. There are a number of ways in which dreams offer help: a voice may confide in us; we may be shown a number of choices, with the most helpful one indicated; we may be told everything is fine and to go ahead with a course of action, or even see the solution to a problem written on a piece of paper.

How do you know if your dream interpretation is correct? This is a question often asked by those new to dream interpretation. If you use the methods set out in this book, you will be following a path thousands of people use and find successful. Moreover, you have the tools for analysing your dreams with you already – the answers lie in your subconscious mind. Working on a dream often brings a tangible sense of recognition. 'Aha, that's what it's about!' my clients say.

As you work through the book, the ways in which you record and interpret your dreams will become more advanced. With practice and dedication, your interpretations will be easier to complete and more profound.

Directing your dreams

As the dreamer, you are the best person to analyse and interpret your dreams. After all, your unique experiences hold the key to their meaning. When starting to interpret your dreams, it can be helpful to view the dream as a play or film and yourself as its director. You choose the characters, the setting and the action – in fact everything in the dream.

Casting your dream

When interpreting your dreams as 'director', first explore the dream's characters in depth, looking at the connections you can make between the dream and your waking thoughts and feelings. Here is an example of how you might work, based on Millie's dream. She wrote,

'I was walking to meet Henry and some other friends. A group of girls walked past me. They wore really high heels and were laughing and joking. I looked down at my flat, plain shoes and felt so boring.'

In order to interpret the dream, Millie broke down the constituent parts. First,

the characters: herself, Henry, a group of girls and their shoes. Next to each character she wrote down any associations that came to mind, without censoring her thoughts. She also thought about events that took place in the days running up to the dream that could have triggered the images. Here's what she wrote:

Henry A friend from school. Fun and reliable, a bit staid sometimes. Yesterday I read an article about Henry Holland, a young fashion designer. He sounded really upbeat and I liked the clothes he was wearing.

Me I feel a bit flat and boring.

Girls They seemed to be having fun and looked cool in their heels. They passed by without noticing me.

So in Millie's account there are two Henrys, both fun, but one a bit staid or boring and one really upbeat. The girls are having fun and are up to the minute in their heels, unlike Millie, whose shoes are 'flat'. When Millie wrote down her associations, she noted that she was feeling a bit low (flat) and wondered if she needed to aim higher in some way, to be more like the 'high' heeled girls having such a good time. She also noticed that the girls passed her by and recognized that she sometimes feels left behind.

Dream settings

The setting also gives you a great deal of information about your dream 'movie'. You may dream of familiar places or of exotic locations you would like to see. Some people dream of weird landscapes, deserted countryside or heaven. Whatever the setting, it carries significant information and holds a clue to the meaning of your dream. If your dream is set in the place you spent your childhood, it may relate to an unresolved issue from that time.

When analysing this element as director of your dream, make another list – this one detailing the places in which your characters appear, and the colours and lighting in your dream settings. Then think about any events, feelings or ideas from that setting that you could usefully reconnect to at this point in your life.

 Work with this exercise now Find a quiet place where you will be undisturbed, then turn to Exercise 5: Interpreting My Dreams on page 66 and follow the instructions.

Meeting dream characters

Psychoanalyst Fritz Perls, who founded Gestalt therapy in the 1940s, worked extensively with dreams. In this form of personal development, the dreamer is encouraged to see all aspects of the dream as part of herself. Perls introduced the idea of using dialogue to investigate dreams. In his method, every part of the dream is given a voice and can speak from its unique point of view. When you take part in a conversation with a frightening part of your dream – with a monster, a savage beast or cruel pursuer, perhaps – you often find that beneath the threatening cloak is a kind, misunderstood character, a modern-day Beast who longs to be understood by Beauty. The part of you that heals and rebalances provides answers to your questions about meaning. So in listening to these different elements of the dream, you may find a way to accept parts of your psyche that previously you had rejected.

You can develop your dream-interpretation skills by trying this self-questioning technique for yourself.

Simply write down your dream, then underline the main characters in the dream, including yourself if you feature in it. Assuming that all parts of the dream represent you, choose one character you wish to communicate with. Now have an imaginary conversation with that character. What do you want to know about this role and what it means to you? Ask questions to clarify things, such as, 'Who are you? Why are you in my dream? What have you come to tell me? What do you want from me?'

You may find it helpful to use the Gestalt empty-chair method. Place two chairs opposite each other: one is for you, the questioner, the other for your character. Sit in your chair and address the character, imagining he or she is seated opposite you. Ask a question. When it is the turn of the dream character to answer your question, move to the other seat. Continue to do this until you have completed your dialogue. After the session, write down any insight you have gained.

Dreaming about yourself

When you dream about yourself, the role you see yourself in will tell you a great deal about what is happening in your unconscious mind. In your dream diary make some notes about whether you are taking action in the dream, or whether you are an observer. Often you will be part of dream scenes taking place in another period in your life or, less frequently, living in a different situation or unknown place. You may be yourself but in a different body or the opposite sex. Note these details down; they provide clues to the underlying meaning of the dream. As you examine each aspect in detail, you can consider what might have triggered the changes in time, location or body.

Sometimes we see ourselves as two different selves in one dream. This can indicate a psychological change. After recording the details in your dream diary, reflect on what the two parts symbolize. Whenever there is a doubling of imagery in a dream, it intensifies the import of the dream.

Everything that has happened in your life may find a way into your dreams. When you are interpreting your dreams, think about recent waking events and the influence they may have had on the movie playing in your dreams, but then let your mind sift through your past to see if events then have relevance for you now.

Christine's past certainly influenced her dreams. 'In my dream, everyone is dead except me. I feel unbearably sad. In another recurring dream I am the dead person and everyone else is alive and they can't see me. But they shiver and turn up their collars when I come near as if I've brought a chill. I shout at them to look at me and speak, but they look through me and shiver.'

This vivid dream started in childhood. Christine's father died when she was six and she and her mother returned to England after living in the United States. Christine's whole life changed: she left friends and the neighbourhood she knew so well to come to an alien land. Such disruption often features in dreams through a lifetime, not only at the time of the event. The sense of isolation is still with her, the dream reflecting not only how invisible she felt at the time of her father's death but during subsequent years, too.

Dreams set in the past may be asking you to revisit old issues. Another client confessed, 'Practically every night I dream of my son as a child and the house I shared with my ex-husband, who is often in the dream too. My son is actually a great worry to us and I feel to blame. Perhaps, in these dreams, where he is a child, I am looking for a second chance to steer him a little better.'

Monster characters

The monster is a ubiquitous figure in dreams. The word derives from the Latin roots *monstrum*, which means divine portent, and *monere*, to warn. This gave rise to the idea that dreams of monsters foretold disastrous events. Dreams of monsters can occur at any age; you may recall dreams from childhood in which you were pursued by ghosts, dragons or terrifying faceless beings. Monsters may combine animal features, devilish creatures and all sorts of harmful characteristics. In a sense our dream monsters amalgamate our internal demons since it is our waking traumas that give birth to our dream monsters.

Victims of war dream of being shot by enemies, Kuwaiti survivors dream of being threatened by Saddam Hussein or pursued by masked paramilitaries, and people who have been raped dream of a dark figure lurking in the shadows waiting to pounce.

Free association

Sigmund Freud is credited with introducing the technique of free association when working with dreams. Try it out as you write about your dreams in order to become better acquainted with your dream characters and the messages they bring. After recording the details of your dream in your journal pages or diary, pick different elements to explore, perhaps a character, setting or action. Put aside your analytic, reasoning mind and simply write whatever comes to mind when you think of this person, place or event without censoring your thoughts. Let your mind freely associate with your fund of memories and past experiences. You may be surprised at how quickly you make connections, understand the motivation behind the dream and recognize its energy. You may unearth very old memories, not considered consciously for years. After thinking about them, can you see that they have pertinent revelations for you now, at this stage of life? Free association frees your subconscious mind to reveal wishes and fears you may ignore in your waking life.

Work with this exercise now Find a quiet place where you will not be disturbed, then turn to Exercise 6: My Dream Characters on page 70 and follow the instructions.

Working with nightmares

It is especially important to pay attention to and interpret nightmares because dreams affect our body chemistry. When we have a frightening dream, the amygdala in the brain perceives it as a real threat, triggering chemical changes that prepare us to deal with that stress by fighting or running away. If this stress reaction is not dissipated, it can damage the body over time.

Once we wake from the dream, it's important to process the threatening feelings to counteract these negative chemical changes. We can do this by paying attention to the content of the dream using the techniques in this chapter – guided imagery, visualization, active imagination. By transforming nightmare images into positive, healing images in this way, we reverse the impact on the body.

Nightmares are sometimes 'wake-up' calls. The fear in the nightmare forces us to wake up in order to escape the terror of being chased, attacked or overwhelmed by a natural phenomenon, such as fire. If you have nightmares, you might consider the fears you have in your waking life and ways in which you could expose them to the light of day rather than keeping them in the dark.

Some triggers

Nightmares are typically caused by anxiety, stress or a major life event, such as divorce or job loss. They are also linked to emotional difficulties, such as bereavement and relationship breakdown, as well as traumatic events like accidents and attacks. Nightmares may be linked to illness and fever or be a side-effect of drugs – for example, L. dopa, used in the treatment of Parkinson's disease, tends to increase the vividness of dreams and the incidence of nightmares, while recurring nightmares are a symptom of Post-traumatic Stress Disorder. Sleep disorders, such as sleep-terror disorder and narcolepsy, can be marked by nightmares, as can the post-surgery recovery period while mind and body heal.

Nightmares often contain information about unresolved issues and may be related to revisiting a stressful event from the past. They weave multiple strands of our experience and fears to form disturbing and distressing scenarios. Dream researcher Ernest Hartmann, Professor of Psychiatry at Tufts University School of Medicine, has made an in-depth study of nightmares and the people who have them. He found that those who are 'nightmare prone' are usually anxious, sensitive beings who have experienced nightmares throughout childhood. They are also more worried about death and their own mortality than other people.

Managing nightmares

We are better equipped to deal with nightmares if we think of them as wake-up calls, drawing our attention to issues we may be suppressing in our waking life. The following practical strategies can be useful in managing bad dreams – I use the word 'monster' here to signify anyone or anything frightening in your dream:

Confront the monster When you are awake, imagine facing the monster chasing you and shout 'Stop!' Then ask why he is bothering you. Ask for the monster's name – the act of naming confers power on the person saying the name.

Draw the monster What could you add to your picture of the monster part of your dream to make you feel safe and contain the monster's energy? Add it to your picture.

Draw/script a response Repeat what you would say to the monster to yourself during the day so that it becomes 'embedded' in your mind. Then you can call on it when you are confronted in a future dream.

Call in a heroic figure Who would you like to help you? Call him or her to your side. It could be a real hero in everyday life or a mythical figure such as Superman or King Arthur.

 Work with this exercise now Turn to Exercise 7: Mastering My Nightmare on page 74 and follow the instructions. If you feel agitated, do a quick relaxation first (see page 16).

 I'm not there yet If you don't yet feel ready to face your demons, don't worry. Return to this exercise at a later date.

Meeting guides and ancestors

In dreams, inner wisdom often surfaces in the guise of a guide, guru, wise person, angelic being or other unworldly form. Sometimes it takes the form of a companion who accompanies you on your dream journey.

You may dream about ancestors who have died many years before or even people you have never met but who have a connection with your family or cultural group. These ancestors may offer advice, warn of dangers or come to console at times of distress. Such dreams are sometimes called 'visitation dreams', when an ancestor offers glimpses of the afterlife (see page 160). Whatever your beliefs about life after death, dreams showing someone who is deceased in another setting allow those who are bereaved to relocate the deceased to a new place. This can help the grieving process and bring great comfort and solace.

Angelic beings

Angelic guides take different forms. They may appear as angels with wings or be formless and ethereal. Sometimes, it is only the voice that the dreamer hears. It is the strong sense that there is a positive spiritual being in your dream that alerts you to such a presence. In most cases they represent spiritual truth or knowledge that we need to reflect on while awake.

Throughout her life, Madeline has experienced dreams that have reflected her spiritual and artistic path and guided her at times of indecision. She says, 'An angelic being appeared by my side in a dream as I was unpacking my bags after a trip to India. "You will not need to return for ten years. You can put those bags away," the voice told me. I saw this as a clear message. And after ten years, when my life had changed, I felt able to return to India and begin another part of my journey to my artistic soul.'

 Work with this exercise now To explore your own experience of meeting a guide in your dream life, turn to Exercise 8: Meeting My Guide on page 78 and locate CD Track 2. Find a quiet place indoors where you can sit or lie down comfortably, have a CD player nearby, then follow the instructions.

DREAM-INTERPRETATION EXERCISES

These exercises will help you to explore your unconscious attitude to dream interpretation and will show you how to gain wisdom from your dream characters. They will also show you how nightmares help you face fears, to enhance your waking life.

Assessing dreams

This exercise investigates your motives for exploring your dreams. You will need a notebook and pen for this exercise. Before you start to think about a dream, write the words 'Dream interpretation' in the centre of a new page and draw seven spokes radiating from the words. Now you are ready to begin.

Exercise 5 INTERPRETING MY DREAMS
CD REFERENCE TRACK 1 (OPTIONAL)

∞ **When to do this exercise** Make sure you can put aside at least 20 minutes to complete the exercise..

- **At the end of each of the seven spokes**, write one word or phrase you associate with dream interpretation. Try not to think too hard; just jot down whatever comes to mind. Clients I work with have written all sorts of words, including 'fascinating', 'hard work', 'scary', 'complicated', 'might not get it right', 'useful', 'mysterious', 'a gift' and 'mining for treasure'.

- **Now, look at the words** you have written down. Do they reflect your views and concerns about working on your dreams? Remember, there are no 'right' or 'wrong' responses to these exercises.

- **Do you want to explore one or more of these words further?** Perhaps they have prompted you to think of more questions. Choose one word to look at in more depth.

- **Write this new word** in the centre of a new piece of paper. Jot down any words or phrases you associate with your chosen word. When you have finished, repeat the exercise again with any other words that intrigue you or seem especially rich in meaning. Then answer the questions on page 67.

My dream-interpretation experience

Questions to consider
How do I feel about dream interpretation?
What can I gain from working on my dreams?
What do I need to do in order to understand my dreams more clearly?

Date _____ Time _____

_____

_____

_____

_____

_____

_____

_____

Date _____ Time _____

_____

_____

_____

_____

_____

_____

_____

Date _____ Time _____

_____

_____

_____

_____

_____

_____

_____

_____

Date _____ Time _____

_____

_____

_____

_____

_____

_____

_____

_____

Date _____ Time _____

_____

_____

_____

_____

_____

_____

_____

_____

_____

Date _____ Time _____

_____

_____

_____

_____

_____

_____

_____

_____

_____

Getting to know your dream characters

Here's your chance to think like the director of a movie. Are the characters in your dream movie all aspects of yourself, and what advice have they got for you at this point in your life? What changes do they indicate? Use this exercise to find out more. You will need your dream diary.

 Exercise 6 MY DREAM CHARACTERS
CD REFERENCE TRACK 1 (OPTIONAL)

When to do this exercise You can do this exercise at any time of the day, just ensure you have at least 20 minutes of uninterrupted time so that you can really concentrate on your dream.

- **Choose a dream**, the more recent the dream, the better. Refresh yourself on the characters, setting and action by reading over the notes in your diary.

- **Now consider the following thought:** what would happen if the main character in this dream intensified his or her actions? How would this affect the other characters in the dream? How does it change the dream? Write down your thoughts.

- **Change the behaviour** of another character from your dream, in the same way. How does this affect the dream and the other characters in it? Now consider the questions on page 71.

My dream-character experience

Questions to consider
How did I feel when I took control of my dream characters?
How do these dream characters relate to different aspects of me?
What information have I learned about them that I can use in my waking life?

Date _____ Time _____

_____

_____

_____

_____

_____

_____

Date _____ Time _____

_____

_____

_____

_____

_____

_____

Date _____ Time _____

_____

_____

_____

_____

_____

_____

_____

_____

_____

Date _____ Time _____

_____

_____

_____

_____

_____

_____

_____

_____

_____

Date _____ Time _____

_____

_____

_____

_____

_____

_____

_____

_____

Date _____ Time _____

_____

_____

_____

_____

_____

_____

_____

_____

Turning negative into positive

This is a technique to help you manage distressing nightmares. Relax before you begin and try not to panic – just give it a try and see what happens. Remember, you are awake and in control. If any unpleasant emotions or memories arise, return your focus to your breath. If necessary, end the session and try again another time. You will need a pen and your dream diary.

 Exercise 7 MASTERING MY NIGHTMARE
CD REFERENCE TRACK 1 (OPTIONAL)

 **When to do this exercise** When you feel relaxed and robust enough to face your demons.

- **Think back to a nightmare from the past.** Think about details — the setting, characters — and the events of the dream.

- **Face the fear**, but keep reminding yourself that you are in your safe waking time now.

- **Now turn all the negative events in the dream into positive events.** Go through the dream section by section, entering each element in your diary as a positive experience or situation. Write using the present tense ('I am', 'She is') in order to maximize the impact of the positivity. To check how you've done, answer the questions on page 75.

My mastering nightmares experience

Questions to consider
How did I feel as I faced the fear?
How did it feel to exert positive control over the dream images?
Do I feel less scared about the nightmare now I have finished this exercise?
How might this nightmare have been a wake-up call?

Date _____   Time _____

_____

_____

_____

_____

_____

Date _____   Time _____

_____

_____

_____

_____

_____

Date _____ Time _____

_____

_____

_____

_____

_____

_____

_____

_____

_____

Date _____ Time _____

_____

_____

_____

_____

_____

_____

_____

_____

_____

Date _____ Time _____

_____

_____

_____

_____

_____

_____

_____

_____

Date _____ Time _____

_____

_____

_____

_____

_____

_____

_____

_____

Finding a dream companion

Many of us meet a dream guide during visualization or meditation. This exercise explores that possibility. As you practise, let whatever grace is offered infuse your mind and body. Remember, dreams come to us for our well-being. Practise in a warm, quiet space where you won't be disturbed.

 ## Exercise 8 MEETING MY GUIDE
CD REFERENCE TRACK 2 (TO FOLLOW THE SCRIPT, TURN TO PAGE 242)

∞ **When to do this exercise** Ideally, you should be relaxed before starting this exercise. You may like to use the relaxation exercise on page 16.

- **Sit or lie down comfortably** and relax. Cover yourself with a light blanket to keep you warm.
- **Read the text** on pages 242–43 and when ready turn on Track 2 and follow the guided meditation.
- **Now consider** the questions on page 79.

My guide-meeting experience

Questions to consider
How did I know that the presence was a guide?
Did I accept the radiant connection that was offered to me?
What does my guide bring me to help me on my path?

Date _____ Time _____

_____

_____

_____

_____

_____

_____

Date _____ Time _____

_____

_____

_____

_____

_____

_____

Date _____ Time _____

_____

_____

_____

_____

_____

_____

_____

_____

_____

Date _____ Time _____

_____

_____

_____

_____

_____

_____

_____

_____

_____

THE LANGUAGE OF DREAMS

The significance of symbols

The language of your dreams may be literal, symbolic, filled with metaphors or mix up all these approaches to understanding. In dreams, everyday objects often carry layers of meaning and are frequently symbolic, standing for objects and ideas that are different from themselves.

A symbol is something that stands for or represents something else, usually by association or social convention. For example, throughout the world a dove is the symbol of peace.

A metaphor is a figure of speech in which a word or phrase is applied to a person or object. It does not literally describe that person or thing, but implies a resemblance. For instance, if we say, 'She is a tiger when it comes to protecting her children', the mother referred to is not literally a member of the cat family, rather she displays attributes usually assigned to big cats. The word 'metaphor' comes from the Greek *metaphora*, meaning 'transfer'. In both the waking and dreaming worlds, metaphors rely for their meaning on our store of associations and network of interconnected images.

Ruby's dream was full of metaphors and wordplay. 'In the dream I couldn't stand up. I was on my knees. My back was against the wall and I was crouching down. I just couldn't move.' When she looked at the metaphors, she asked herself who she couldn't stand up to, and what, or who, in her waking life, made her feel like cowering. She also asked herself why she was on her knees, a colloquialism for a person who is worn out.

Interpreting symbols

Throughout history, symbols, like dreams, have been interpreted according to the traditions of each culture, influenced by religious beliefs, spiritual practices and social conventions. The swastika, for example (from Sanskrit roots meaning 'well-being' and 'luck'), was for early Hindus a symbol of a positive life force and joy. That was how the symbol was regarded until sullied by Nazi Germany, where it was adopted as a symbol of the regime.

In the 20th century, psychoanalyst Sigmund Freud focussed the interpretation of symbols on sexual symbolism. In his *Tenth Introductory Lecture* (1916), he listed 30 symbols for male genitalia and more than 20 for female genitalia. For phallic symbols, he included revolvers and umbrellas – objects that expand or burst out like the male orgasm. Symbols for female genitalia include vessels, cupboards and vases, since the vagina 'contains' the penis. Subsequently, there has been a wider reading of the meanings of the huge variety of symbols in our dreams. Later dream researchers like Carl Jung felt that Freud overemphasized the sexual symbolism in dreams. In reality, we each bring our own personal symbolism to our dreams. If I dream of a dog I generally see it as a positive symbol because I like dogs, but if someone were afraid of dogs or had a cultural aversion to them, then a dream dog would be a negative symbol.

 Work with this exercise now Turn to Exercise 9: My Symbol Immersion on page 98 and follow the instructions.

 I'm not there yet You might find it useful to look at some images in my book *The Mystic Symbols*, which is filled with symbols from around the world and covers all major religious, architectural, esoteric and magical symbolism.

Understanding archetypes

Swiss psychotherapist Carl Jung developed the idea of psychological archetypes. Found in the dreams, art, literature, fairy tales and myths of all cultures, archetypes are common expressions of being shared by people throughout history and seem to come from the deepest part of the unconscious mind. Jung called this inheritance of the collective experience of humankind the 'collective unconscious'. There are four main archetypes, which often appear in our dreams: the Anima and Animus, the Shadow and the Self.

The Anima and Animus

The Anima represents the feminine element in men, and the Animus the masculine aspect in women. Each of us has masculine and feminine energy, though sometimes one or the other is repressed. Dreams offer the repressed aspect a chance to surface, bringing about balance. Lia explained to me how her dreams helped her: 'Recently I've had recurring dreams of an affair with a male friend. I'm only just realizing he is another aspect of myself. He is always the nice guy, never gets angry or feels

down, never shows much emotion and is always ready to please. This is the "front" I put on while I'm silently seething inside at all the injustice around me.' Now she has identified her Animus, or masculine energy, how does Lia use this information? 'I now try to do what I want to do rather than what I should do. It's been a real transformation.'

In order to achieve psychological balance we need to accept the whole of our nature. Jung defined an individual who balanced their feminine and masculine aspects well as Syzygy, or the divine couple, which represents wholeness and completion. Dream researcher and psychotherapist Carol Warner described a series of dreams involving her Animus, in which she watched this balance restore itself. She dreamed of being in a 'mail' room and the play on the words 'mail' and 'male' helped her to realize that she needed to bring about some changes that allowed her masculine energy – more assertive and career driven – to be incorporated into her feminine side. We all have masculine and feminine energy, the Anima and Animus, and as with the energy of *yin* and *yang*, when it is balanced we are healthier.

The Shadow

Dreams incorporating our Shadow may reveal elements of ourselves that are dormant or hidden, only emerging out of the dark as we dream. The Shadow symbolizes primitive, animal-like instincts, or the less restrained, wilder parts of our nature that may cause us discomfort. This may be the angry, malicious, vengeful or predator part

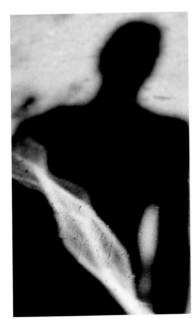

of ourselves which we cannot reveal because we fear disapproval from others. For example, if you dream of a murderer, you might explore his motivation by considering his point of view. Have a conversation with him (see pages 56–57). What does he say? What is life like from his point of view and what justification, if any, does he give for his behaviour? Does this reveal some murderous feelings you have?

Sometimes we project our Shadow on to someone else. For example, we may deny our own feelings of aggression, but attribute them to the enemy – an assailant who attacks us in our dreams, or the snarling nightmare hyena who would tear us to pieces. Psychologist and author Robert Van der Castle says that the Shadow in our dreams is the same sex as the dreamer.

The Shadow side of ourselves is a valid part of each of us, allowing us to acknowledge the intensity of our emotions without having to act them out. The very process of recognizing them often dissipates their energy and frees us to use our energy more positively. Exploring our Shadow elements in this way allows us to absorb them and become more whole.

The Self

Jung regarded the Self not just as the individual but as a larger, transcendental totality – God, or the element within each of us connected to all living things, the earth and the universe. This larger Self 'binds' together our conscious and unconscious selves. We discover this 'higher' self when all our potential and every aspect of our lives become united, a process Jung named 'individuation'. The Self expresses the unity of our personality as a whole.

Other archetypes

Jung described many other subsets of archetypes, some of which may appear in your dreams and fantasies, and in stories you are drawn to. Think about movies such as *Star Wars*, *The Wizard of Oz*, *The Lion King* and the *Harry Potter* series, and you will spot these archetypes. They are frequently the stuff of our dreams, reflecting personal situations in archetypal form.

Family archetypes include the Father, a powerful authoritarian and rule-enforcer, the Great Mother, who is nurturing, protecting and soothing, and the Divine Child, a transformational power that propels us toward personal growth and individuation.

Story archetypes include the characters often found in fairy tales and mythology: the Hero, a courageous rescuer and champion of the underdog. Think of St George and the dragon or David and Goliath. Then there is the Maiden, defined by her purity, innocence and naivety. The Wise Old Man is known for his guidance, ancient wisdom and fortitude, while the Magician is a figure of power who has unseen connections with other realms. The Witch has magical powers that can be dangerous or facilitate rescues, while the shape-shifting Trickster is deceptive, changeable and shamanistic.

The shape shifter is an archetype of transformation or metamorphosis, changing from human to beast, from friend to lover, from angel to devil. Werewolves are popular movie examples of shape-shifting, *wer* meaning 'man' in Old English. The shape shifter carries the duality of nature and expresses the conflict we feel in controlling our wilder selves in society. The need for change and disguise is seen in waking life in dressing up – in burlesque clothes or at a masked ball we can reveal another aspect of our nature.

The hero's journey

Joseph Campbell, the 20th-century mythologist, identified a story line in all these archetypal scenarios which he named the 'hero's journey'. The hero must encounter danger and overcome it, he has usually been separated from his parents or guardians and has a quest to fulfil. On such journeys there are encounters with adversaries, helpers or rescuers, magical creatures and shape shifters who transform from one person to another or from human to animal form.

Your dreams may take this form, too. You may undertake quests or missions and have to find your own heroic self to overcome the obstacles facing you. To

do this it is helpful to cultivate *philoxenia* love of the stranger. The opposite of xenophobia, it represents openness and acceptance. Practise this skill by welcoming the archetypes that appear in your dreams, whether beautiful or bestial. Like Beauty, in the story of Beauty and the Beast, you may find that below the frightful exterior lies a heart of gold. Maintaining the attitude of the Divine Child archetype – finding grace and joy in any situation – can lead to important personal transformation.

To explore a dream using this method, retell it as a fairy tale. Start with the words 'Once upon a time', choose the main characters and capitalize their names. Make the setting more extreme or dramatic, and exaggerate as many other aspects as you can; something small becomes minuscule, anything large gigantic. This includes gestures, movements and weather. Add 'blanket terms' – 'always', 'never', 'every' – and dialogue. End with a saying or moral. Now read your personal fairy tale. How does it fit the hero's journey? What is your quest, what obstacles have you overcome and who has helped you? Think about yourself as the hero. Celebrate the strengths that have brought you so far.

 Work with this exercise now Turn to Exercise 10: Re-entering My Dreams on page 102 and locate CD Track 3. Have a CD player nearby, then follow the instructions.

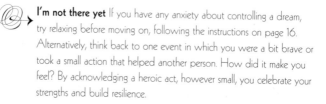 **I'm not there yet** If you have any anxiety about controlling a dream, try relaxing before moving on, following the instructions on page 16. Alternatively, think back to one event in which you were a bit brave or took a small action that helped another person. How did it make you feel? By acknowledging a heroic act, however small, you celebrate your strengths and build resilience.

Alchemy and dreams

The process of dreaming is akin to alchemy, the aim of which is to transform the impure to the pure on an inner level and to transmute base metals, such as lead, into gold. As we go through life, many of us work to refine our base characteristics and develop our higher nature, perhaps to reach spiritual enlightenment or wholeness, – the process Carl Jung calls individuation (see page 86). Our dreams reveal the alchemical changes taking place within us through the language of alchemy, which is the language of symbols.

In dreams, as in alchemy, it is helpful to view events as processes rather than single situations. Esme's dreams were full of alchemical imagery and symbols. She told me, 'Behind a fireplace in our lounge, I discovered a secret compartment. A small, exquisitely shaped apartment completely hidden from the world. It had a glorious carpet, an oven and a small sunny greenhouse extension. There I was in it. I felt whole. I felt whole because I was alone, complete, not missing anyone. I sat comfortably enclosed in my secret compartment.'

The dream, coming after a series of dreams based around the themes of fire, destruction and trauma, confirmed Esme's growing sense of personal strength and completeness. She is shown her 'inner room', symbol of the alchemist's 'inner' work, in which she has engaged over many years. She has found a secret space to nourish herself physically and spiritually. The greenhouse, place of natural growth and productivity, symbolizes her continuing growth and development as she journeys on her path to individuation.

Symbols of rebirth may emerge as you become more aware of your life path, or soul journey. An inner friend or enemy may show you a different way to behave or new ways of thinking. Alchemists referred to this as 'a certain one within', who could be asked questions. The answers brought about transformation. A cave is a well used symbol of a place of rebirth, according to Jung a secret place in which someone can be incubated and renewed. It is in the darkness of the cave, as in the unconscious, that knowledge can be found. Such dreams give us another way of knowing.

Embracing your power animal

There is a hidden language of animals, birds and fantasy creatures in our dreams and they are important teachers. In our dreams animals bring us what we lack and guide us to a deeper awareness of ourselves and the world we live in. For example, when they fly these animals reveal the connection between the higher self, or spiritual world, and the waking world.

Throughout history, wise men and women, shamans and mystics have developed their intuitive skills by seeking and embracing a power animal. Also known as a totem animal or medicine power, the animal, such as a wolf or bear, lends the individual the collective strength, wisdom and knowledge of that whole species or genus.

In the Native American vision quest tradition, a shaman would meet an animal with special importance in a vision; the power animal then shares its qualities with the shaman. It often also has magical qualities, such as the ability to talk or fly, which the shaman adopts to travel between worlds.

You may meet your power animal in a dream or visualization. Sometimes it will appear threatening and you may feel under attack, as Sally did when a bear circled her house in a dream, trying every door and window to reach her. Often this threatening aspect comes at a time when your unconscious is trying to break through, to force you to recognize something you are overlooking when awake. A bear symbolizes protection and nurturing, because the mother bear is fiercely protective of her young. When Sally had this dream her sister had died and she was trying to cope with her grief alone; she needed someone to care for her and recognize her pain, as a loving mother would. The bear, far from threatening her, was symbolically trying to nurture her.

If you dream of a threatening animal, as Sally did, use the dialogue techniques on pages 56–57 to help uncover the important message the animal is bringing you. Think about the positive qualities the animal has, and reflect on how you could incorporate them into your life.

Finding your power animal

You can identify your power animal in a number of ways. Perhaps a certain animal is a recurring visitor to your dreams or so vivid and potent that when you wake it is imprinted in your memory. If you find yourself thinking about the dream animal during your waking hours, take it as an indication that this animal has significance for you. Sometimes, you will find that an animal you dreamed of appears in your waking world, in a piece of jewellery or on a billboard, in a magazine or on television. Use such synchronistic occurrences as prompts to think consciously about the animal, give it space in your mind and heart, and accept the gifts it offers.

 **Work with this exercise now** Turn to Exercise 11: My Power Animal on page 106 and follow the instructions.

Universal dream themes

A number of universal themes occur in dreams throughout the world and across cultures. Carl Jung explained that they form part of mankind's collective unconscious. On the following pages you will find a list of the most common dream themes, with explanations that reveal their symbolic significance in your own life.

Being pursued

Pursuits in which the dreamer is under threat of some kind are a common dream theme. Since the beginning of history humans have had to avoid danger from wild animals and from strangers who belong to other clans or tribes. Today those fears are as widespread as ever. One present-day pursuit dreamer told me, 'I dream of driving a car. Another car is following me and I'm afraid they'll catch me.' Another said, 'I was in large ferry boat. Women were chasing me. I got away by splitting myself. They grabbed me but didn't know it was me. At the same time I saw myself hiding in a corridor.' Later the second dreamer admitted that she was anxious about the dream part of her that

had been left behind. If you have dreams in which you are fleeing danger, think about what may be threatening you in your waking life. What are you running away from?

Falling

Common in all age groups, falling often symbolizes insecurity, lack of support and feeling helpless. It may show your feelings about losing status – perhaps being demoted at work or within your social circle. When you are falling in a dream, it may be because you lack balance and need to become more grounded in your waking life. There is a common myth that if you fall in a dream and hit the ground you will die. I can assure you this is not true!

Flying

The experience of flying in dreams is usually exhilarating and brings a sense of power and control. It often comes in lucid dreams (see pages 220–23), where the dreamer can travel to any place she chooses. As you fly in a dream, you rise above a situation and have an enhanced viewpoint. It may be that you are too

close to a situation in your waking life and need to get some distance so that you can see more clearly. On the other hand, when you take off and truly fly, you may be accessing your real potential; your dream is affirming that you are reaching new heights.

Being naked or in the wrong clothes

Wearing the wrong clothes, or clothes that do not cover you adequately, may reveal a fear of being judged negatively. You feel that you don't live up to the expectations of others and are exposed in some way. Often these dreams – and others in which you are naked – are set in public arena, which make you feel isolated and embarrassed. Being naked gives the dreamer no protection from outside scrutiny, unlike our clothes, which we choose to reflect our public persona. If such dreams cause you distress, think about who is present in the dream and ask yourself whether you reveal too much to them.

Being lost or trapped

When you are lost or trapped in a dream, you have a lessened sense of control. You are not in command of the situation and may lack clarity. Being lost may symbolize that you lack direction

in life and need to take time to reflect on what you have lost and what to do to recover what is missing. You may feel trapped by present circumstances and need to find new outlets to return you to an authentic path. Such dreams may also reveal that your energies are blocked or trapped in some way; you need to take action to clear those blockages.

Testing situations

Many people dream of being back at school taking exams only to realize that they have revised the wrong subject, the topic is one they have never studied, or they are in some other way completely unprepared to take the test. These dreams often come at testing times in life, for example, before job interviews or during a difficult phase of a relationship. If you have these dreams, consider the demanding situations in your waking life and whether you are feeling more stress than you admit.

Unable to complete/frustration

Frustration dreams often involve machinery or electronic goods, such as mobile phones that do not connect. One dreamer told me, 'A recurring theme is that I am travelling and never quite get there. Trains don't move or I lose my luggage.'

Katy told me her dream: 'I was on a motorway, but there were no cars. I was running trying to get round on the hard shoulder. There were blind people. A blind man got hold of me and said I'm going to tell you if you are going to go blind or not. I said I didn't want to know. I was wearing mittens because I didn't want him to see my palms because he might read my future. Then I'm running on the motorway, getting nowhere.'

The dream may show part of you that you need to bring back into balance. This dream reflects Katy's waking anxiety. She admitted, 'I do have a fear of illness, especially mental illness. My sister has ME and her sight is affected. I'm scared of that happening to me.'

 Work with this exercise now Turn to Exercise 12: My Universal Dream Theme on page 110 and follow the instructions.

SYMBOLS AND THEMES EXERCISES

These exercises will show you how to understand the
incredible power of dream symbolism and how to re-enter
your dreams in your waking hours to take them to higher
levels of awareness.

Understanding my dream symbols

This dream symbol exercise helps you to start thinking about the objects that appear in your dreams as symbols and to build a rich store of personal meanings to help you interpret them. It is particularly helpful if you are puzzled by something in a dream. You will need your dream diary.

 ## Exercise 9 MY SYMBOL IMMERSION
CD REFERENCE TRACK 1 (OPTIONAL)

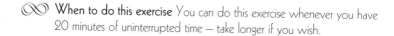 **When to do this exercise** You can do this exercise whenever you have 20 minutes of uninterrupted time — take longer if you wish.

- **Sit comfortably** and go back through your diary to find a dream to explore. From within this dream select a key object or action. This is your symbol.

- **Close your eyes** and contemplate your chosen symbol. Allow your unconscious freely to explore the symbolic meanings attached to it. Words, thoughts and images will emerge. Let them — don't try to control your mind.

- **Open your eyes** and write down all the thoughts and meanings that occurred to you. Now answer the questions on page 99.

My symbol-immersion experience

Questions to consider
What themes emerged as I meditated on my symbol?
How does this symbol enrich my waking life?
How could I include this symbol in my waking life to deepen my connection with it?

Date _____ Time _____

_____
_____
_____
_____
_____
_____

Date _____ Time _____

_____
_____
_____
_____
_____
_____

Date _____ Time _____

_____

_____

_____

_____

_____

_____

_____

_____

_____

_____

Date _____ Time _____

_____

_____

_____

_____

_____

_____

_____

_____

_____

_____

Date _____ Time _____

_____

_____

_____

_____

_____

_____

_____

_____

Date _____ Time _____

_____

_____

_____

_____

_____

_____

_____

_____

Activating the imagination

Dream re-entry, or active imagination as Carl Jung called it, is a way of using guided imagery to carry on a dream in a controlled way from the point where it ended. The key is first to settle yourself into a calm, reflective state, and then to think about the ending of a dream and imagine how it might continue. Practise in a calm, quiet place where you will not be disturbed.

 Exercise 10 RE-ENTERING MY DREAMS

CD REFERENCE TRACK 3 (TO FOLLOW THE SCRIPT, TURN TO PAGE 243)

When to do this exercise Ideally, you should be relaxed before starting this exercise. You may like to use the relaxation exercise on page 16.

- **Settle yourself** in a comfortable sitting position. Make sure you are warm enough.
- **Read the text** on pages 243–44 and when ready turn on Track 3 and follow the guided meditation.
- **Now consider** the questions on page 103.

My dream-re-entry experience

Questions to consider
How did it feel to tap into my hidden potential?
Did I enjoy the feeling of control?
Have I turned my negative experiences or stumbling blocks into stepping stones
that will help me move forward?

Date _____ Time _____

_____

_____

_____

_____

_____

Date _____ Time _____

_____

_____

_____

_____

_____

_____

Date _____ Time _____

_____

_____

_____

_____

_____

_____

_____

_____

Date _____ Time _____

_____

_____

_____

_____

_____

_____

_____

_____

_____

Date _____ Time _____

_____

_____

_____

_____

_____

_____

_____

_____

_____

Date _____ Time _____

_____

_____

_____

_____

_____

_____

_____

_____

_____

Meeting an animal

In this exercise you take notice of animals that seem prominent or recur in your dreams. They may be alerting you to characteristics it would be useful for you to embrace. You will need your dream diary.

 ## Exercise 11 MY POWER ANIMAL
CD REFERENCE TRACK 1 (OPTIONAL)

 When to do this exercise Practise whenever an animal seems significant in your dreaming or waking hours or when you would like to change your life.

- **Leaf through your dream diary,** noticing dreams that feature an animal, bird or fantasy creature. If you have not dreamed of an animal recently, pick an animal that appeals to you at the moment.

- **Ask yourself what you most admire about this animal** — let your mind run free with the possibilities, however odd they might seem. Then make a list of the animal's characteristics.

- **Look at the list** and jot down ways in which you could use some of these attributes to your advantage. Try to apply them in your everyday life.

- **When you have finished,** consider the questions on page 107.

My power animal experience

Questions to consider
What positive energy and strengths does my power animal bring to me?
Why do I need these strengths now?
How can I develop more of these positive qualities to enhance my waking life?

Date _____ Time _____

_____

_____

_____

_____

_____

Date _____ Time _____

_____

_____

_____

_____

_____

Date _____ Time _____

_____

_____

_____

_____

_____

_____

_____

_____

Date _____ Time _____

_____

_____

_____

_____

_____

_____

_____

_____

Date _____ Time _____

_____

_____

_____

_____

_____

_____

_____

_____

_____

Date _____ Time _____

_____

_____

_____

_____

_____

_____

_____

_____

_____

Exploring common experiences

We share dream motifs across the centuries and cultures. This exercise allows you to explore the individual meanings for you within a universal theme. It is helpful if you have recurring dreams of a universal dream theme. Acting as an objective observer can offer great insight into what this dream is telling you and gives you some distance from the dream so you can see its meaning more clearly.

 ## Exercise 12 MY UNIVERSAL DREAM THEME
CD REFERENCE TRACK 1 (OPTIONAL)

 When to do this exercise You can do this exercise whenever you have 20 minutes of uninterrupted time — take longer if you wish.

- **Begin by looking back** at the universal themes described on pages 92–96, from flying to appearing naked in public. Choose one that you have experienced in a dream.

- **Now allow yourself to view the dream as if it were a movie.** You are not emotionally involved in the action, but simply an observer. 'Watch' the movie from beginning to end.

- **Having watched the action,** ask yourself the questions on pages 111. They will help you to understand the relevance of this common human experience to your own life.

My universal dream theme experience

Questions to consider
How might my past have brought about this universal dream theme?
What would I change in this dream?
How can I change my waking life to help me learn from this theme?

Date _____ Time _____

_____

_____

_____

_____

_____

_____

_____

Date _____ Time _____

_____

_____

_____

_____

_____

_____

_____

Date _____ Time _____

_____

_____

_____

_____

_____

_____

_____

_____

_____

Date _____ Time _____

_____

_____

_____

_____

_____

_____

_____

_____

_____

DREAMS AND CREATIVITY

The creative energy of dreams

Dreams can spark a galaxy of creative impulses within us. Each dream represents a potential seed of creativity and every dream a new experience, even if the theme is familiar. Dreams have a natural energy, atmosphere and suspense all their own. By drawing from our subconscious and unconscious, they give our conscious minds access to an unlimited supply of new ideas. Dreams can become a basis for a novel, poem, TV script, piece of visual art or a scientific theory.

Dreams may give you signs relating to your destiny by revealing unknown aspects of your character or bring you into contact with a person who symbolizes what you are becoming. It is up to you to integrate what you learn in your dreams into your waking life, honouring the insight dreams bring you. The psychotherapist Carl Jung did this and confided in his autobiography that everything he accomplished in his life – all his works and creative activity – was contained in his 'initial fantasies and dreams' dating from 1912, though at first these were only 'emotions and images'.

Creativity lies at the heart of all discoveries. The desire to know how something works – to understand our material and spiritual worlds – has spurred on scientists as well as artists. Indian mathematician Srinivasa Ramanujan, famous for his ability to devise complex mathematical formulae, said that throughout his life he was assisted by the Hindu goddess Manakki. She would appear in his dreams and present him with a mathematical formula, which he would verify on waking.

Dreams that impress

The term 'extraordinary dreams', coined by American dream researcher and parapsychologist Stanley Krippner, refers to dreams that reflect not only our day-to-day life, but have a creative component. They may spawn an idea, provide insight into new areas or even prepare us for the future. Such dreams impress us because they are so unusual, beautiful and highly memorable. They are the 'big' dreams we cannot forget. Jung calls them numinous, sacred or mystical, dreams.

Frank Gehry, one of the world's most acclaimed architects, is best known for the Guggenheim Museum in Bilbao in the Basque country. He designed his first British building after one such powerful dream. His friend Maggie Keswick Jencks founded a series of centres for cancer care after being diagnosed with breast cancer. Gehry said, 'I dreamt about Maggie constantly. I wanted to do justice to Maggie's vision for the centre. The whole process was intuitive.' The third Maggie's Cancer Caring Centre in the UK was built in Dundee in 2003. Gehry added, 'What came out of that intuitive, dreaming process is as good as anything I've done, including Bilbao.'

To explore your most powerful dreams, choose one dream from the past that has stayed with you throughout your life. Revisit the dream in detail. Try to feel the emotional impact it had on you and think about the insight or wisdom it brought you. Drawing the dream can help capture its vivid nature. Having reminded yourself of the details and emotional impact, ask yourself what effect it has had on you and the life choices you have made.

 Work with this exercise now Turn to Exercise 13: My Creative Release on page 130 and locate CD Track 4. Find a quiet place indoors where you can sit comfortably, have a CD player nearby, then follow the instructions.

Writers and dreams

Many writers reveal that their work originated in dreams. Romantic poet Samuel Taylor Coleridge said that his poem 'Kubla Khan' was almost dictated to him, word by word, in a dream. Also in the 18th century, writers Voltaire (in France) and Goethe (in Germany) told of poems originating in their dreams, like John Bunyan's earlier allegorical journey *Pilgrim's Progress*. If you've ever been terrified by the story of *Frankenstein*, you might not be surprised to learn that it sprang from a nightmare. Mary Shelley, its author, woke in terror and told her husband about her terrifying dream. He encouraged her to develop the idea. It became her first novel and has not been out of print since its first publication in 1818.

Writers frequently use events from dreams to inspire a plot or invoke characters. Indeed, novelist Graham Greene became so immersed in the life of his fictional characters, that in the second instalment of his autobiography he admitted dreaming his characters' dreams, complete with their memories, symbols and associations. William Styron dreamed the idea for *Sophie's Choice*, first published in 1979, which became an award-winning film. American author Sue Grafton says that the most memorable of her dreams are quite dark and concern being menaced by something outside her house. She attempts to lock every opening to keep out the menace, but it looks around and sees another place it could enter. Readers will recognize this sense of threat from her alphabet mysteries, which began with *'A' is for Alibi* in 1983. The dream initiates the idea and the artist brings it to life in the waking world.

The Danish writer Hans Christian Andersen was inspired by the legend of 'the dream god' Ole-Luk-Oie, the sandman who blows fine dust in children's eyes until their heads droop and he can tell them 'pretty stories'. In the myth, Ole-Luk-Oie, or Old Lukoie, carries an umbrella under each arm. One is adorned with pictures while the other is plain. He twirls the first umbrella over good children to reward them with colourful dreams. But if a child has been naughty, uses his other umbrella to bring

dark, dreamless sleep. Andersen kept a dream journal between the ages of 20 and 70, and used his dreams as sources for stories such as 'The Princess and the Pea', 'The Steadfast Tin Soldier' and 'The Snow Queen'. As Patricia Garfield, celebrated dream researcher, notes, 'understanding Andersen's dreams gives us a window into the creative mind and helps us see how we can use our own dreams to enrich our productive lives.'

Robert Louis Stevenson's novella *Strange Case of Dr Jekyll and Mr Hyde*, first published in 1886, sprang directly from a dream. In 1892, Stevenson wrote in 'A Chapter on Dreams' about the relationship between his dreams and his writing: 'I can but give an instance or so of what part is done sleeping and what part awake... I had long been trying to write a story on this subject... For two days I went about racking my brains for a plot of any sort; and on the second night I dreamed the scene at the window, and a scene afterwards split in two, in which Hyde, pursued for some crime, took the powder and underwent the change in the presence of his pursuers. All the rest was made awake, and consciously...'

Stevenson saw this as his greatest work and it was an instant bestseller. Stevenson used dreams extensively and named his dream creative team 'The Little People' or 'my Brownies', referring to the supernatural creatures of British lore who do good deeds in secret by night. Sometimes, he said they told him the story piece by piece; on waking all he had to do was get it down on paper.

Some dreamers worry that they can't do anything creative with their dreams because they only remember a snippet, but this is not the case. Dr Jill Mellick, psychologist, writer and dream worker, explains one approach in *The Natural Artistry of Dreams*. Imagine that the fragment of your dream – a shoe, part of the body, an aspect of a building – has been painted by an artist and enlarged to an image measuring three metres (ten feet) square. It is hanging in a famous gallery in prime position. Now, ask yourself a few questions. What does it look like? How do you feel about it? What resonates with you? This approach helps shift your viewpoint and allows you to expand your interpretation. It also encourages your creative self to expand to a much greater scale.

Writing creatively

Argentinian writer Jorge Luis Borges, famed for his use of 'magic realism', said 'Writing is nothing more than a guided dream'. You may want to use your dreams as Robert Louis Stevenson did (see pages 118–19), as a jumping off point for creative writing. I've certainly used this approach in my own writing and teach it on creative writing courses in Europe and the United States. One useful approach is to think of your dream as a movie. You are the producer, the casting director, the actors, set designer, scriptwriter, costume designer and editor. In fact, you are in control of the whole dream and can develop it in any way you choose.

From dream to page

Choose a vivid dream and give it a title. Then consider the main characters in the dream – they will play the leads

in your movie. In order to give them some substance and hold our interest, have a conversation with them. Ask each one, 'Who are you? What mood are you in? What are you doing now and what have you done in the past?' Choose one element of the dream and magnify it. Let your imagination soar, ignoring the inner critic who seeks to stifle your creativity. Let's look at this example for inspiration, written by my client Helen. She gave it the title 'My Dream House'. Notice that it is written in the present tense.

'I am walking up to a lovely cottage. A man opens the door, smiles at me and says, "I'm really pleased you could make it." He guides me through the house, showing me the rooms as if I were buying the house from him. "You'll be very happy here," he says. "We love it, but it's time for us to move on." Suddenly, I see a pregnant woman, who is obviously his partner or wife. Then both figures disappear and I am left exploring the house on my own.' Helen's dream ended there.

Who is in the dream? In this example, Helen, the dreamer, and a man and woman. The couple don't have names, so we named them Carl and Janine.

I asked Helen to take a leap of imagination and let her characters introduce themselves, writing down the responses without censoring her thoughts. She wrote this:

'Hi, I'm Carl. I've lived here at Farfields Cottage for six years and it's great. Well, it was great until I was made redundant. I've not been able to find another job here so we've got to sell up. I've found a new job in Dubai. Janine's not that happy because she's finally pregnant and I'm having to leave. I'll be back for the birth, then Janine will join me in Dubai. She's moving in with her Mum until the baby's born, which is good because she's been acting strangely since she got pregnant.'

'My name is Janine Clark. I'm 26, five months pregnant and thrilled that we finally made it. I thought I'd have to have IVF, but then, when we'd given up hope, I found out I was expecting. It's brilliant. The downside is that Carl has to work abroad and we've have to leave this house. In a way, I'm glad to be going because for the last few months, I've been hearing a weird crying outside the back door at about 10 o'clock at night. Carl says I'm just imagining it. To be honest, I think something is stalking the

house, if a house can be stalked. I hope the girl who wants to move in will cope here on her own.'

So Helen has the starting point for a short story, novel or screenplay here. Given this example, she could be in for a dark time in her 'dream' house. To increase the plotting opportunities, she could add what writer Stephen King calls a 'What if?' situation to her basic outline. What if Janine has developed clairaudience, the ability to hear more than Carl? What if this stalking creature follows her to her mother's home? What if she starts dreaming of events that begin to happen? The possibilities are endless.

Developing ideas

There are many other ways to develop the basics that come to you in dream form. You might try some of these practical techniques:

More characters Add another character to the dream drama.

Plot prompts Write a letter to one of the dream characters to move the narrative along.

Stir it up Include 'What if' situations, as described above.

Introduce magic An element like an animal that can talk or a genie who can grant three wishes takes your work into another realm.

Add a dramatic twist Perhaps your dream character is confronted by a threatening robber or is told she has won the lottery.

Change the ending Make up a new, perhaps more literary ending to replace the end of your dream. Dramatize it so it has greater inpact.

 Work with this exercise now Turn to Exercise 14: A Letter to Me on page 134 and follow the instructions.

Discovery and dreams

The unconscious solves problems. Think about the 'tip of the tongue' phenomena – the sense that you almost have the answer to a question, but it is just eluding you. As you focus away from the answer with a shrug, your unconscious mind whirrs into action, seeking the answer.

The dreaming mind is constantly putting this process into action; it is part of the continuum of communication that runs from waking thought to dream experience. Nothing is ever forgotten. Though we may not be able to remember items of information on demand, all our experiences, knowledge and history are stored in the brain. Dreams mediate between the conscious mind and those 'forgotten' aspects.

Our dreaming self continues to seek a solution to a creative problem as we sleep. While we are awake, thinking about the subject that puzzles us, we 'prime the pump', making ready the next phase of activity required to resolve the problem or initiate an action. While we sleep we continue to work toward the solution, which is why dream 'incubation' is so productive.

The Nobel Prize winning scientist Albert Einstein said that dreams were the basis for every discovery he made. They intrigued and inspired him to discover the secrets of the universe. The German chemist Friedrich August von Kelkule recalled a dream in 1865, which brought about a scientific revolution. As he slept, his brain continued working on a problem which had been puzzling him for years – how benzene molecules held together. In his dream, the scientific structures he'd been wrestling with transformed into snakes that swallowed their tails. On waking, he realized that the benzene compound was not an open structure but formed from closed chains, just like his dream snakes. Unlike many other scientists of his age, Kelkule was convinced of the extraordinary power of the dreaming mind. When he received a major scientific award, he concluded his speech with the words, 'Let us learn how to dream, gentlemen, and perhaps we will discover the truth.'

The Russian scientist Dmitri Mendeleyev carried out research into how chemical elements could be categorized according to their atomic weight. The solution evaded him until one night, he said, 'I saw in a dream a table where all the elements fell into place as required. Awakening, I immediately wrote it down on a piece of paper. Only in one place did a correction later seen necessary.' The message in all these stories is that if you want to harvest your problem-solving skills, keep your dream diary beside you every night.

Artists and dreams

The 19th-century British visionary painter, Pre-Raphaelite, Sir Edward Burne-Jones was described as a 'Victorian Artist-Dreamer'. He said of his work that it was 'a dream, a noble dream' and his letters are filled with accounts of his dreams. His wife, Lady Burne-Jones, confirmed that throughout his life he was a dreamer of dreams by night as well as by day. Burne-Jones's highly charged erotic dreams allowed his passionate sexuality free rein at a time of Victorian prudery.

His paintings are filled with Jungian archetypes (see pages 84–87): heroes on quests such as in his Perseus series of paintings and his many paintings and drawings of Cupid and Psyche, used to illustrate a folio edition of William Morris's *Earthly Paradise*. Burne-Jones's works correspond closely to the archetype of the hero called to adventure who journeys away from his home, faces adversity, slays dragons or defeats enemies and is finally rewarded with the hand of the maiden or the throne to a kingdom. The 'Briar Rose' series of paintings he worked on from 1871–90, based on the story of Sleeping Beauty, also carry symbols of his dream world and the mythic hero's quest to rescue the trapped maiden.

The Spanish Catalan surrealist painter Salvador Dalí would sleep under a bright light, after finding that this heightened the visual imagery of his dreams and gave them an intense vibrancy. His 1931 painting 'The Persistence of Memory' with its soft, melting watches is a wonderful example of his dream-inspired work. So too is French artist Henri Rousseau's 'The Dream', from 1910. With its wide-eyed lion, naked reclining woman and exotic jungle foliage, all lit by a white moon, it has the air of being conceived in a dream, which it was.

Film-making too, has been inspired by dreams. Swedish director and screenwriter Ingmar Bergman and Italian director Federico Fellini are celebrated for the dream-like quality of the imagery in their movies. In fact Bergman said all his films were his dreams.

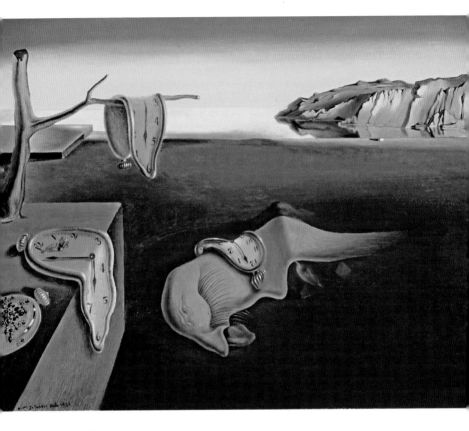

Work with this exercise now Turn to Exercise 15: Dreaming for
My Art on page 138 and follow the instructions.

Musicians and dreams

In 1714, the Italian composer Guiseppe Tartini was commissioned to write a sonata, but couldn't come up with any ideas. One evening while walking along a moonlit beach he spotted a glass bottle. Something drew him to it and when he looked closer he saw the devil trapped inside. The devil said he would do anything Tartini wanted if only he would release him from the bottle. Tartini asked him to write a sonata and, once the devil had agreed, released him. The devil played a diabolically fast melody and when he finished Tartini woke up. Immediately he transcribed the music, which came fully formed, and the 'Devil's Trill' violin sonata, as it is often called, has remained popular since.

Other composers have shared similar revelations from the world of dreams. In the 1850s, Richard Wagner said he dreamed the whole of his opera *Tristan und Isolde*, while songwriter and Hollywood lyricist Paul Webster, who wrote 'Love Is A Many Splendored Thing' and 'The Twelfth of Never', always took a pen and paper to bed because his dreams were a constant source of inspiration.

The tradition continues in the world of rock and pop. The beginning passage of a tune woke Rolling Stone star, Keith Richards. He got up and recorded it – now recognized worldwide as the opening of '(I Can't Get No) Satisfaction'. Similarly, Sir Paul McCartney dreamed the tune of 'Yesterday'. The dream was so vivid that when he arrived to rehearse with the Beatles, he thought they had already been playing it. He was shocked to learn that the other members of the band had never heard the tune. Many other people immersed in a creative life find that the brain continues to work on musical ideas during the night.

 Work with this exercise now Turn to Exercise 16: My Dream Music on page 142 and locate CD Track 1. Find a quiet place indoors where you can lie down comfortably, have a CD player nearby, then follow the instructions.

CREATIVITY EXERCISES

These exercises will help to release blocks that are holding back your creative spirit and allow you to fully appreciate the characters who appear in your dreams. You will gain greater clarity into your expanding creative processes.

Releasing creativity

This visualization exercise uses a crystal to help unblock your creative energy. Pick one of the crystals from page 23 that appeals to you and cleanse it (see page 22) before starting the exercise. The day after practising the exercise, cleanse it again. This exercise is also helpful if you are suffering from writer's block.

Exercise 13 MY CREATIVE RELEASE
CD REFERENCE TRACK 4 (TO FOLLOW THE SCRIPT, TURN TO PAGE 245)

∞ **When to do this exercise** Practise this visualization when you wish to connect with and develop your creative potential — perhaps if you need new perspective at work or clarification of ideas when studying.

- **Sit comfortably** in a place where you won't be disturbed.

- **Read the text** on pages 245–46 and when ready turn on Track 4 and follow the guided meditation.

- **Now consider** the questions on page 131.

My creative release experience

Questions to consider
What creative issues am I looking for help with?
How do I feel about my creativity now?
How could my dreams assist me?

Date _____ Time _____

_____

_____

_____

_____

_____

_____

Date _____ Time _____

_____

_____

_____

_____

_____

_____

Date _____ Time _____

_____

_____

_____

_____

_____

_____

_____

_____

_____

Date _____ Time _____

_____

_____

_____

_____

_____

_____

_____

_____

_____

_____

Date _____ Time _____

_____

_____

_____

_____

_____

_____

_____

_____

Date _____ Time _____

_____

_____

_____

_____

_____

_____

_____

_____

Writing a character

Use this exercise to flesh out the cardboard cut-out characters that appear in your dreams. You will need your dream diary. It will allow you to get to know the people who appear in your dreams with greater depth and clarity.

Exercise 14 A LETTER TO ME
CD REFERENCE TRACK 1 (OPTIONAL)

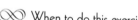

When to do this exercise This is useful if you feel stuck with a piece of creative work, as well as for revealing insight into your dreams.

- **Look back at your dream diary** and select a dream containing a character who puzzles or intrigues you.

- **Visualize that character,** picturing how he or she looks and speaks, and his or her mannerisms. Include the tiniest details of dress and gait. Try to get under the skin of your character.

- **Now ask that character to write a letter to you,** telling you who he is and why he has come to you at this point in your life. Write the letter on your character's behalf. What kind of handwriting would he have and what expressions would he use? To explore the insight this gives, answer the questions on page 135.

My letter to me experience

Questions to consider
How did writing the letter increase my understanding of my dream?
What message did the letter deliver to me?
How does this character contribute to my wholeness and well-being?
How would I respond to this letter if I were to write a reply?

Date _____ Time _____

_____

_____

_____

_____

_____

Date _____ Time _____

_____

_____

_____

_____

_____

_____

Date _____ Time _____

_____

_____

_____

_____

_____

_____

_____

_____

_____

Date _____ Time _____

_____

_____

_____

_____

_____

_____

_____

_____

_____

Date _____ Time _____

_____

_____

_____

_____

_____

_____

_____

_____

Date _____ Time _____

_____

_____

_____

_____

_____

_____

_____

_____

_____

Dreaming for art

In this exercise you use your creativity to enter the dream world of a character in a work of art. This visualization is a way of deepening your understanding of character and expands your creativity You will need pen and paper.

Exercise 15 DREAMING FOR MY ART
CD REFERENCE TRACK 1 (OPTIONAL)

 When to do this exercise Make sure you are fully relaxed before beginning the exercise. You may like to use the relaxation exercise on page 16.

- **Find a postcard of a painting** or choose an illustration in a magazine or book showing a character, animal or object. Any image that appeals to you is right for this exercise.

- **Once you feel relaxed**, focus on the image and allow yourself to be drawn to one of the characters, animals or objects.

- **Now imagine that character or object is dreaming.** Without analysing your thoughts, write down that dream. To reflect on the experience, answer the questions on page 139.

My dreaming for art experience

Questions to consider
What drew me to this image?
How did it feel to dream from a different point of view?
What was the message of the dream?
How can I integrate part of this dream experience into my life?

Date _____   Time _____

_____

_____

_____

_____

_____

Date _____   Time _____

_____

_____

_____

_____

_____

Date _____ Time _____

_____

_____

_____

_____

_____

_____

_____

_____

Date _____ Time _____

_____

_____

_____

_____

_____

_____

_____

_____

_____

Date _____ Time _____

_____

_____

_____

_____

_____

_____

_____

_____

Date _____ Time _____

_____

_____

_____

_____

_____

_____

_____

_____

_____

Composing dream soundtracks

This exercises allows you to capture the atmosphere of a dream in a soundscape. Start by switching off your thoughts and lulling your body into a state of relaxation by listening to Track 1 of the CD.

Exercise 16 MY DREAM MUSIC

CD REFERENCE TRACK 1

When to do this exercise This can be useful for relieving stress and when you are looking for creative inspiration.

- **Sit or lie down comfortably** (see page 16) and when you are ready, turn on Track 1 on the CD player and listen to the relaxing sounds until you feel calm and present. Notice any areas of your body that are tense and consciously relax them.

- **Once you feel that your mind is quiet** and your body relaxed, think about your dreams. Which ones have a similar atmosphere to the sounds you have been listening to? Choose one dream in particular.

- **When the track ends**, play it again if you would like to continue the exercise.

- **Now try to identify some pieces of music** that would make a good soundtrack to your dream. If you are musical, compose a piece to highlight the themes of the dream. If you prefer working with words, write the lyrics for a dream song.

- **When you have finished,** consider the questions on page 143.

My dream music experience

Questions to consider

What music came to mind as I thought about my dreams?
How did the music I chose or made reflect the mood of my dream?
Does this music make me feel connected to other people, places or events?

Date _____ Time _____

_____

_____

_____

_____

_____

_____

Date _____ Time _____

_____

_____

_____

_____

_____

_____

Date _____ Time _____

_____

_____

_____

_____

_____

_____

_____

_____

_____

Date _____ Time _____

_____

_____

_____

_____

_____

_____

_____

_____

_____

_____

BE YOUR OWN
DREAM HEALER

Healing dreams

I believe that most of our dreaming is a form of healing. Our dreams ask us to look at every part of our existence – physical, emotional, spiritual and practical – and to reflect on the lives we lead, aspects of ourselves that need to change, and our relationships with others.

In the Indian healthcare tradition, Ayurvedic practitioners use dreams as part of the diagnosis process. So do doctors of Traditional Chinese Medicine (TCM). In the classic text of TCM, *The Yellow Emperor's Classic of Internal Medicine*, whose knowledge has been handed down over four and a half millennia, the Emperor brought attention to the significant connection between dreams and illness. Homeopathy practitioners across the Western world would concur, taking dreams into account when taking a case history and making a diagnosis. The dreams may be divided into classes corresponding to organs of the body.

In recent years in the United States, Dr Larry Dossey has advocated using dreams in everyday medical diagnoses and to speed recovery from illness. Another American MD, Dr Bernie Siegel, an oncology surgeon, has explored the powerful role the mind can play in fighting illness and says it is vital to listen to a patient's dreams. Deeprak Chopra, doctor, visionary and author, also confirms the importance of including dreams in medical diagnoses and treatment plans.

The dreaming mind is sensitive to subtle changes in the body. Before our waking mind realizes there is a health problem, the dreaming mind can alert us. Toni told me, 'I keep dreaming about hands near my throat or dreams in which I'm reaching for my throat.' Then one night, in a dream the hands touched her throat and she spotted a small lump that her doctor later diagnosed as a thyroid tumour. If you feel pain in dreams, notice where it is located and when you wake up check your body for physical problems. For reassurance, you might like to book an appointment with your doctor.

Dr Oliver Sacks, bestselling author and professor of neurology and psychology,

regards dreaming as a barometer of neurological health and disease. He relates how people who suffer from frequent migraines often have intense dreams of fireworks or light changes before an attack. One of his patients knew he would have a seizure because his usual black and white dreams were suffused with red.

Dreams sometimes give information to aid recovery, too. Dr Sacks was recovering from a leg injury but having problems mastering the change from a pair of crutches to a single stick. In his dreams he saw a way to successfully make the switch and when he woke tried the dream technique, filled with confidence it would work. It did.

How it works

In the mid-1900s, Vasily Kasatkin, a psychiatrist at the Leningrad Neurosurgical Unit in Russia, studied the content of more than 10,000 dreams from 1,200 subjects. The patients had a range of disorders, from minor infections to life-threatening tumours.

He found that illness increased the patients's ability to remember their dreams and the content often vindicated a later clinical diagnosis. Themes included battles, war, conflict, raw meat, dead people and dirty water. As patients recovered, their dreams became more pleasant, while those whose condition deteriorated reported more disturbing dream imagery.

Kasatkin thought of dreams as sentries watching over our health. Nerves come to the brain from every part of the body, he explained, relaying signals of impending illness that the subconscious translates into dreams. So our dreams act as an early warning system. Dreams of a chest wound, for example, would come before a heart attack. One of Kasatkin's patients had a dream of a crab clawing at her stomach. She was later diagnosed with stomach cancer and recalled that the crab is the astrological sign for Cancer.

The study of psychoneuroimmunology (PNI) shows just how well the mind,

body and spirit are interconnected. The work of pharmacologist Dr Candace Pert has shown that neuropeptide receptors in the brain connect all systems in the body, including the immune system. Every emotion we feel involves the release of neuropeptides, which impacts on our physical well-being. Our dreams reflect these emotional states and we can use them to become more aware of the links between mind and body. According to this theory, blocked emotions impact negatively on the immune system and make us more susceptible to illness, so in order to increase the efficacy of the immune system we need to free emotional blockages and find constructive ways to express our feelings.

Exploring the connection

If you would like to try out these thoughts, think back to a dream you have had that captured your feelings about a difficult issue in the past. This might be a problematic relationship, a painful separation, failed expectations or a health concern. Try to remember the emotional tone of the dream and your feelings and responses to it on waking and in the days that followed the dream. Notice how your body responds when you remember the dream. Then take a calming deep breath and let go of the negative feelings. If it helps, visualize the negativity leaving your body as you exhale. As you inhale, allow yourself to experience forgiveness. Visualize the ties that bind you to these negative emotions loosening. How does this make your body feel? Picture yourself being free and able to let go of the negative thoughts connected with your dream. What can you do now to increase these feelings of forgiveness and release during your waking hours? Cherish yourself as you let go of painful attachments.

 Work with this exercise now Turn to Exercise 17: My Healing Visualization on page 162 and locate CD Track 5. Find a quiet place indoors where you can lie down comfortably, have a CD player nearby, then follow the instructions.

 I'm not there yet If you find thinking about trauma, illness or past hurt too difficult at the moment, follow the relaxation exercise on page 16 and return to this at another time.

Real dream-healing experiences

For many years I presented an annual workshop entitled Greet The Dream Healer for people with cancer and their family and carers. One year Irene came and talked of the only dreams she could remember. They were utterly black; there was no light and she was filled with terrible despair. She confided that two years previously her husband had died and then, to her utter dismay, her 19-year old son had killed himself. Irene was bereft, only just managing to get through each day. I showed her ways in which she could work on her dreams and accept and transform the devastating feelings they expressed.

The following year Irene returned to the workshop saying, 'I had to come back and talk to you because my dreams have helped save me. I wanted to show you this dream.' Irene presented her drawing of a glorious rainbow. She was standing on the left-hand side of the rainbow, and at the bottom of the rainbow on the right-hand side were two figures, her husband and son. She said, 'I can reach them in my dreams now. We haven't talked yet, but we will.' She was reconnected with her beloved family by a symbolic rainbow bridge between heaven and earth.

In a dream group made up of women with cancer, many shared dreams that reflected their fear as they waited for test results. The most significant dreams related to anxiety about the re-emergence of cancer when they were in remission. Talking about their dreams helped these women to express their concerns and share their common experiences. Dreamwork also helped women to adjust later, as they went through reconstruction surgery. One woman dreamed of cradling her reconstructed breast and singing a lullaby to it – it was wearing a baby's bonnet. This was a profoundly healing experience for her.

Understanding the significance

Sometimes the symbols in a dream may be hard to interpret. Distance can help

us to get the message and telling a dream from another point of view can bring profound insight. For example, Diane had this dream: 'I was driving my old car down a curious underpass and ended up in a cul-de-sac with high walls and no space for turning. My children were in the car with me, though they are grown up now.'

Changing her point of view to that of an observer she said, 'There's a woman driving a car through a kind of tunnel. She comes into a road with walls so high she can't see over them. She comes out into a road that has no way out so she has to turn back. It's a tricky manoeuvre because she's not got much space. The children in the car are distracting her, which makes it more difficult for her to turn around.'

By taking this other viewpoint Diane could see how hemmed in she felt and frustrated. She saw that her life was taking wrong turnings and seemed blocked, with no way out. She had been refusing to look at this, pushing the feelings 'underground' and passing them off as unimportant. The appearance of the children symbolized a time in her life when she had little time for herself because of the responsibility of caring for them. After dreams like this, you might ask yourself how you can spend more time nurturing your well-being.

 Work with this exercise now Turn to Exercise 18: Drawing My Body on page 166 and follow the instructions.

Diagnostic dreams

Dreams about illness that occur before you see symptoms of an illness or health concern in your waking hours are known as 'prodromal' dreams. The word comes from a Greek word *prodromos*, meaning 'running before'. Diagnostic dreams may offer you literal or symbolic indications – a concern about melanoma, for example, might show up as a mole on your dream body that is highlighted in some way or an animal mole which is active in your dream.

Keeping a prodromal dream record

Jana from Solvenia contacted me because she wanted to share two important dreams. I believe they have important messages for other pregnant women and so I include them here. Jana wrote:

'In spring I became pregnant and was looking forward to having a baby. Then at nine weeks I had this dream: there is a herd of cattle in a meadow with a bull. Its belly is torn and it is bleeding, its intestines hanging out. I don't know if there had been a fight. The message seemed to be one of violence (though not directed toward me) and of loss. When I woke up, I was worried. Soon I started bleeding and in the twelfth week I miscarried. The doctor told me the foetus had died at nine weeks. I guess, the death was simultaneous with the dream.

'A year ago, four years after the miscarriage, I became pregnant again. I was scared and a big black bull reappeared in my dreams. This time though, he was perfectly healthy and strong, even dangerous. I dreamed he was circling the house I was hiding in. I didn't dare come out, I was afraid he

would hurt me. When I woke up I thought: this is a little threat. I began bleeding, but only a little. My doctor said the baby was doing just fine but I was still anxious.

'At five months I had another dream: I am walking with a relative who lives in the country. It's harvest time. The colours are beautiful, the sun is shining and there is a feeling of overwhelming abundance. We come to a barn. There is a single grape attached to it, a dark indigo colour, ripe, very beautiful and big and placed unusually high. I look up and say, "You didn't pick this one?" "No," she says, and adds firmly, "We'll leave it until autumn so that it ripens."

'When I had my baby girl in August, you can imagine, I cried. As I've been writing this I realized that partly because of this dream, we named our daughter Visnia, meaning not only "of/from the sky" but also "sour cherry", like the dark grape of the dream.'

Reading the dream

The initial dream of the bleeding bull can be seen as prodromal; it comes before Jana has any indication that she will begin to bleed and lose the embryo she is carrying. The bull often symbolizes male energy, the Animus (see pages 84–87), and because it is wounded here, suggests that Jana might not have integrated this energy into her life. In the second dream, the male strength is there but, while still threatening, is not damaged. In the last dream we read an affirmation that the grape is firmly attached and ripening. This is further emphasized by the relative, the wise woman, telling Jana that it must be left until fully ripe. In Jana's first two dreams, we can see that one part of her was aware that her pregnancy was not proceeding well. The third dream is much more positive and confirmed for her that she would deliver a healthy baby.

Many dreams during pregnancy reflect anxieties about birth and the health of the baby. These are perfectly natural and such dreams give vent to feelings that are often suppressed during the day. If you are pregnant and having disturbing dreams, talk to your midwife or doctor. Chat, too, to other pregnant women at antenatal appointments; you will probably find that you are not alone in your dreams. You might like to look at my book *Venus Dreaming*, which has a section on dreams in pregnancy as preparation for childbirth.

Dreaming and anxiety

Research indicates that 60 per cent of the content of dreams reflects anxiety. The dominant emotional concern of the dreamer guides and determines the content of your dream, so if you are feeling vulnerable, run down or fearful, this emotion will be echoed in your dreams. Dreaming of cancer may not be prodromal (see pages 152–53), but rather a reflection that you are concerned about your health, feel life is out of control, or you are unable to maintain boundaries and feel invaded by current events.

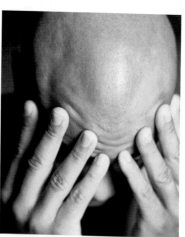

Anxiety in a dream usually indicates that important, and perhaps threatening, ideas are coming from your unconscious. The anxiety is a signal that you need to shine some light into this area. Though you might be fearful, only by facing the fear can you dissipate it. There are many examples of people who are going through an extremely difficult time emotionally whose dreams led them to recovery.

Jody's early dreams were full of dark threat. She explains, 'I've suffered from depression for the last eight years. Often in these dreams there is a sense of darkness in the background, which I assume is my depression, but it isn't fearful or threatening. Rather it feels like a warm, protective blanket.' She was surprised that her depression – which she finds awful – should come across as protective. By addressing this, she discovered that her depression has prevented her from having to deal with difficult people at work.

Becca's dream has all the hallmarks of a dream associated with depression:

'I dream of being stuck under a grey, flat thing. I'm up to my neck. I asked my daughter to pull me out, but I knew she was too little to help. It's frightening; I can't get myself out of my situation. I've no leverage. I'm so flat, so low, that I can't lift myself out.' In her dream, Becca is stuck, the tone is grey and lifeless and she uses the words 'flat' and 'low', which are often used to describe a depressed mood. Clearly, as her dream shows, Becca needs help from an adult rather than her daughter, who is too immature to get her out of this situation.

Common signs:

People going through a difficult emotional time frequently dream of floods or tsunamis, and of being carried away by water. It is as if their dream self has been inundated with feelings and no longer has any control. And because no one can hold back the waves, the dreamer is in danger. If you are having this type of dream and have not experienced a flood in waking life, think about what is happening in your life that is threatening to sweep you away or overwhelm you.

In the story of the flood which appears in many cultures as well as in the Old Testament, water covers the entire earth so that everyone but a small band – such as Noah and his family in the Bible – die. Symbolically, it ends the old world, washing away everything so that mankind can make a fresh start. If your dreams echo this, consider whether you need to make a complete change in your life, particularly if you feel stuck in a rut and are feeling unhappy.

Sonia told me about her dream, 'I have been under great stress recently. I dreamed I had a snake wrapped around each of my ankles and feet and I found it difficult to walk. Later the same night I dreamed I was in a basement and even though I could see the steps leading to the inside of the house, I could not get to them.'

As is evident from her dream. Sonia, like Becca, is stuck. She wants to get to the house, often a symbol of the self, but cannot reach it. What's more she is 'tied down' by snakes. Snakes symbolize renewal, since they regularly shed their old skin. They are also related to spirituality and healing. The caduceus, the age-old symbol of healing, is made up of two snakes wrapped around a staff. For Sonia, who feels she can't make changes to alter her 'crazy situation' as she calls it, the dream is showing her that healing and transformation are possible. Taking action in her waking life

may enable her to take those first positive steps.

Drugs and dreaming

The sedative drug morphine is named after Morpheus, the Greek god of dreams, so it may come as no surprise to learn that our dreams can be altered by the substances we ingest. Medication, herbs, food, dietary supplements, non-prescribed drugs and alcohol all affect our dreams and nightmares. Beta-blockers prescribed for patients with heart problems may increase nightmares. Medication that affects levels of the neurotransmitter seratonin, such as drugs commonly used to treat depression – fluoxetine (trade name Prozac), citalopram (Celexa) and mirtazapine (Remeron) – can cause odd and disturbing dreams. Hypoglycemia, low blood sugar, may also lead to nightmares. An increase in disturbing dreams can also be caused by rapid withdrawal from different substances. If you are troubled by nightmares and are taking medication, talk to your doctor. Your nightmares may be a side-effect of the drug, and alternative medication may be prescribed.

 Work with this exercise now Turn to Exercise 19: Easing My Anxiety on page 170 and follow the instructions.

Incubating healing dreams

Dream incubation (see pages 30–32) has the potential to provide profound insight into your self and your life. It can also be used in healing. The ancient Greeks believed that each person carried within themselves the knowledge of their own cure, which could be accessed in dreams. Medical incubation, in which guidance or healing were sought, was widespread in ancient Greece.

Galen (born 129 CE), physician to the gladiators and five Roman emperors, emphasized the need to observe dreams carefully for clues to healing. He used them to diagnose illness and to determine which remedies would be most effective in bringing about a cure.

If you have a prodromal, or diagnostic dream (see pages 152–53) that alerts you to a possible illness, use the incubation exercise on pages 174–76 to ask your subconscious 'What should I do about it?' A treatment-directive healing dream may follow. These give information or

ideas about what treatment may ease your discomfort. They may tell you what foods to eat and exercise to take, indicate changes to the way you lead your life or point out useful complementary therapies. Some dreams help to bring about healing by rebalancing mind, body and spirit, offering a holistic approach to enhance your health and well-being. Sometimes the healing offered in these dreams comes from a figure you trust with your health, such as a doctor, an angel or a spirit guide (see pages 64 and 90–91). Do book an appointment with your doctor, too, to check the diagnosis.

 Work with this exercise now Turn to Exercise 20: My Healing Request on page 174 and follow the instruction.

Dreaming to enhance well-being

As well as physical ills, dreams can alert us to psychological, spiritual and relationship problems that we may not be fully aware of when awake. Simone, for example, had recurring dreams of falling off cliffs. When she thought about these dreams, in which there was no support beneath her feet and nothing to hold on to, she realized they reflected feelings of insecurity. Since her relationship with her boyfriend had ended unexpectedly, she felt 'the ground has gone beneath my feet'. In her dreams, the metaphor of falling conveyed that sense of having no firm foundation in life. She practised making positive affirmations to build a sense of security, and after repeating them for seven days before falling asleep, she no longer fell off the cliff in her dreams. As her confidence increased, Simone still saw the same setting in her dreams, but instead of falling saw herself confidently looking out into a vast landscape that offered limitless possibilities.

We can use such dream imagery in many waking activities, from imagining new futures for ourselves to drawing or writing stories. To enhance the experience, start by getting yourself into a meditative state of mind by following the relaxation exercise on page 16. Once you are relaxed, use all your senses – touch, taste, sight, hearing, smell – to inform your drawing, writing or imaginary scenario. Wherever possible give your intuitive self the opportunity to contribute to the healing imagery. For example, if you are thinking about a rainbow as a healing image, you may have a flash of inspiration that you need to surround yourself with those colours. Trust your intuitive self and gather together scarves or swatches of material and hold them or place them where you will see them as you move about your home. If an animal that symbolizes healing has appeared in your dreams and you feel you need more of its energy, trust that instinct and cut out images of this animal from magazines to make a collage.

Coping with loss

The death of a loved one affects us on many levels, physical, emotional and spiritual. Following bereavement, our immune systems can be compromised, making us more susceptible to infection and illness. Dreams can help us move to a different phase of life after a special relationship has ended so sadly.

Continuing relationships

Our dreams continue the bonds we have with those we love. The psychiatrist Dr Elisabeth Kübler-Ross, a pioneer in working with terminally ill patients who established the five stages of grief model, advised that if we want to see our loved ones in dreams, we should make a request to see them before going to sleep.

Paul Lippmann affirms this thought in his 2006 paper on dreams, 'The Canary in the Mind' in *The American Journal of*

Psychoanalysis. He states, 'If one can see with one's own eyes, in a dream, one's own dead father or grandmother or dead infant or dead enemy, then surely they have not disappeared in death, only changed form. Thus, after death, some essence of the dead must still exist.'

Robin Gibb, singer and songwriter, was part of The Bee Gees, a multi-award winning group. After his brother died suddenly in a routine operation in the United States, Robin had recurring dreams of his dead sibling. He told me, 'Maurice, Barry and I would be together, after a practice or rehearsal then it was time for us to leave. Maurice would be sitting in an armchair. I'd say, "We're going now," and he'd say, "Why can't I come?" It was as if he didn't know he was dead.'

The dream was upsetting and Robin struggled to understand it. However, he came to the conclusion that Maurice died so unexpectedly that he did not have time to accept that he was dead. Also, it was such a shock for the remaining brothers who had spent almost every day with each other, that they too found it hard to believe he was truly dead. The dead stay with us in our dreams.

Deathbed dreams and visions

People on the verge of death often 'see' apparitions of the dead coming to meet them in order to accompany them to the other side. Research in the 1960s by Dr Karlis Osis of the American Society for Psychical Research and by Professor Erlender Haraldsson, Emeritus Professor of Psychology, University of Iceland, found that such visions were a cross-cultural phenomenon. Such 'visitation' dreams often bring great solace.

Many years ago when my mother was dying, she dreamed about her own mother coming to visit her. My mother told me, 'She had her hat and coat on and said, 'Come on, May, we'll be going soon.' My mother was overjoyed by the dream of her mother who had died fifty years before. Over the next two weeks, my mother spoke about many such dreams, in which her mother was coming closer and indicating that they would leave together soon.

Two days before my mother May died, she had a joyous dream that filled her with light. Her father had died in World War I at Ypres in France when she was a small child and she had hardly seen him. In this last moving dream she said. 'My father came into the room. He said, "Me and the bride have come to take you now, May. It's time." They were both smiling and it was so lovely to be with them again.' My mother was comforted and uplifted by this dream and died peacefully a short time later.

Etta was very young when she had her first mystical experience. She said, 'When I was about six, and in hospital dying from unknown causes, I had a vivid dream. I came to a large black door which opened as I approached. I walked through. At the time I realized I was 'at death's door', but was undisturbed by the fact. When I went through it was dark and blurry, but I was aware of a feminine presence. I was also aware that though I had stepped through the door, everything did not end and that I had a very important decision to make: should I continue or turn back? I was curious but decided to go back. The next day I began to recover.' Etta found the experience comforting. Since that dream, she has no doubt that there is an afterlife and no fears about death.

HEALING
EXERCISES

These exercises will show how dreams can bring balance to your whole being, connecting mind, body and spirit through visualization. They also give you the opportunity to ease anxiety through drawing and dream reflection.

Working with your dreams

In this healing visualization exercise you work with the connection between your body and mind, relaxing and allowing your dreams to bring you back into a state of balance and wholeness. It helps to be fully relaxed before you start so first follow the relaxation exercise on page 16.

 ## Exercise 17 MY HEALING VISUALIZATION
CD REFERENCE TRACK 5 (TO FOLLOW THE SCRIPT, TURN TO PAGE 246)

When to do this exercise Try this when you would like to free yourself from negativity and whenever your mind and body seem out of balance.

- **Lie comfortably** on a bed or exercise mat. Cover yourself warmly.

- **Read the text** on pages 246—47 and when ready turn on Track 5 and follow the guided meditation.

- **Now consider** the questions on page 163.

My healing visualization experience

Questions to consider
How did my body sense the healing energy?
What specific request for healing did I make?
What symbols of transformation have my dreams shown me?
How can I stay on the path to inner transformation?

Date _____ Time _____

_____

_____

_____

_____

_____

Date _____ Time _____

_____

_____

_____

_____

_____

Date _____ Time _____

_____

_____

_____

_____

_____

_____

_____

_____

Date _____ Time _____

_____

_____

_____

_____

_____

_____

_____

_____

_____

_____

Date _____ Time _____

_____

_____

_____

_____

_____

_____

_____

Date _____ Time _____

_____

_____

_____

_____

_____

_____

_____

_____

_____

Dream enhancement

This dream practice works to enhance your dreams. It boosts well-being and allows you to understand the drives that influence your dreams. You will need a sheet of plain paper and some coloured pencils or crayons. Work in a quiet, comfortable space where you will not be disturbed.

 Exercise 18 DRAWING MY BODY
CD REFERENCE TRACK 1 (OPTIONAL)

∞ **When to do this exercise** Try this if your dreams are disturbing or you are facing illness or loss.

- **Sit quietly** and make yourself comfortable. Think back to a dream that relates to your mental or physical health. It may concern the whole of your body, a specific part or be mainly about the thoughts in your head.

- **Remind yourself** of the tone and mood of the dream by contemplating the details for a while.

- **Now pick up a pencil or crayon** and draw an outline of your body on the paper. Alternatively, just draw your head or whichever part of your body relates to your dream and your thoughts about it.

- **Without pondering** too much, add colours and patterns to your outline. You may want to add words too. Do whatever feels right and don't censor any thoughts or impulses. When you have finished your picture, record your impressions on the pages that follow.

My drawing my body experience

Questions to consider
How did I feel when I drew my body?
What key colours and patterns did I include in the picture?
What information can I take from this exercise?
What does this picture tell me about how I might heal myself?

Date _____ Time _____

_____

_____

_____

_____

_____

Date _____ Time _____

_____

_____

_____

_____

_____

_____

Date _____ Time _____

_____

_____

_____

_____

_____

_____

_____

_____

_____

Date _____ Time _____

_____

_____

_____

_____

_____

_____

_____

_____

_____

Date _____ Time _____

_____

_____

_____

_____

_____

_____

_____

_____

Date _____ Time _____

_____

_____

_____

_____

_____

_____

_____

_____

Alleviating anxiety and depression

By using this exercise you can gently explore the reasons why you may be feeling anxious or depressed, and start to lift your mood. Your dreams can help you take these first steps in self-healing. You will need your dream diary.

 ## Exercise 19 EASING MY ANXIETY
CD REFERENCE TRACK 1 (OPTIONAL)

∞ **When to do this exercise** Try this practice when you feel down or stuck in some way, and would like to explore the power of dreams to lift you and help you take the first steps in a positive direction.

- **Sit quietly** in a place where you feel safe and make yourself comfortable. If it helps, calm your mind and body by following the relaxation exercise on page 16.

- **Think about your dreams** Choose a dream which featured anxiety or depression as a theme. This may be in the content or in the emotional tone. In your diary write down what you think was causing your anxiety or low mood.

- **Now picture your dreaming self.** Imagine he or she can give a gift to the dream and its characters to lift their mood. You can give anything at all; everything is possible. What will you give? Write it down now.

- **When you feel ready,** bring your thoughts back to the present and write down your thoughts following the questions on page 171.

My anxiety-easing experience

Questions to consider
What did I feel when I had the power to give any gift to alleviate the anxiety?
What changes happened in the dream once I had given my gift?
What gift could I give myself to bring more balance into my life?

Date _____ Time _____

_____

_____

_____

_____

_____

_____

Date _____ Time _____

_____

_____

_____

_____

_____

_____

Date _____ Time _____

_____

_____

_____

_____

_____

_____

_____

_____

Date _____ Time _____

_____

_____

_____

_____

_____

_____

_____

_____

_____

Date _____ Time _____

_____

_____

_____

_____

_____

_____

_____

_____

_____

Date _____ Time _____

_____

_____

_____

_____

_____

_____

_____

_____

_____

Bringing about healing dreams

In order to incubate a healing dream, practise this exercise during the day. Before you go to sleep, repeat the request. When you wake up, write down the dream you have incubated and reflect on its meaning.

 Exercise 20 MY HEALING REQUEST
CD REFERENCE TRACK 1 (OPTIONAL)

 When to do this exercise Practise during the day, then repeat when you go to bed.

- **Lie down comfortably** in a quiet space, making sure that you will not be disturbed. If you find it useful, relax your mind and body by following the relaxation exercise on page 16.

- **Imagine you have an invisible scanner** that can highlight areas of physical and emotional discomfort. Scan your whole body slowly and methodically.

- **Make a mental note** as you scan your body of any points of tension, discomfort or stress. Include any physical changes or unusual sensations as you continue this scan.

- **When you have finished** the body scan, allow your attention to come back to the room in which you are lying. Gently bring yourself to a sitting position then ask yourself the questions on pages 175. Don't forget to repeat the answer to the final question to yourself before you go to sleep tonight.

My healing request experience

Questions to consider
What did I learn from scanning my body?
How can I use this knowledge to incubate a dream?
What request would I make when asking for a healing dream?
How could I word this request in a clear, positive way?

Date _____   Time _____

_____

_____

_____

_____

_____

_____

Date _____   Time _____

_____

_____

_____

_____

Date _____ Time _____

_____

_____

_____

_____

_____

_____

_____

_____

Date _____ Time _____

_____

_____

_____

_____

_____

_____

_____

_____

_____

PSYCHIC
DIMENSIONS
TO DREAMS

What are psychic dreams?

The word 'psychic' refers to that which is outside the possibilities defined by the laws of physics, for example, knowing that your friend has had an accident when you have not been informed in the usual way. I had a dream that my sister, who lived thousands of miles away, was terribly ill and I later found out that she was in hospital. There was no logical way I could have that information, but a psychic connection told me she was in danger.

'In antiquity, there was no people and practically no individual who did not believe in divine revelation through dreams.' stated the French historian of astrology Auguste Bouché-Leclercq. Indigenous Australians have inhabited the Dreamtime dimension since arriving on the continent some 40–70,000 years ago. The Dreamtime explains the creation of the world, the landscape and the laws of physics, and is continued to this day in a 'Dreaming' enacted through ritual. In the Dreamtime, people dream toward the future and wait for the future to dream back to them. In this way, they subtly change the future in the way they communicate to it.

Psychic phenomena have intrigued and baffled mankind for centuries. Dating back to around 2,000 CE, the Egyptian papyrus of Deral-Madineh reveals examples of divine revelation and oracular dreams taken into consideration when decisions were made on matters of state. The Egyptians also tried to communicate with others via dreams, an early recognition of telepathy, believing that homeless spirits carried messages from one dreamer to another. There are at least 70 references to dreams and visions in the Bible, while in ancient Vedic literature, dreaming was regarded as an intermediate state between this world and the next, where the soul could roam.

Edgar Cayce, an American psychic and healer, said, 'Dreams work to solve problems of the dreamer's conscious waking life. And they work to quicken in the dreamer, new potentials which are his to claim.' He believed that dreams bring us information from our higher selves; from what he called the 'super-conscious' level, the wise self we may ignore while awake.

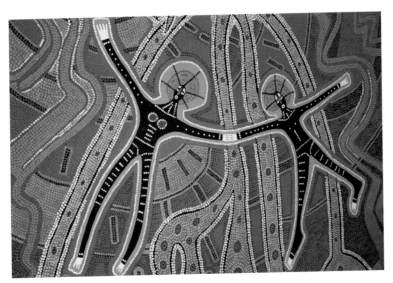

Types of psychic dreams

Also known as 'psi' dreams, psychic dreams take a number of common forms:

Precognitive dreams Foretell future events as yet unknown to the dreamer.

Telepathic dreams Involve communication across distances, usually with those with whom we have a strong emotional bond.

Divinatory dreams Bring contact with a divine being or spirit. These types of dream experiences usually involve visual or auditory experiences.

Astral travel Allow the dreamer's 'subtle body' to explore other places and dimensions.

Most psychic activity in dreams relates to precognition, prophecy and clairvoyance and often concerns those to whom we are close. As my fellow dream researcher Rosemary Ellen Guiley says, 'We are linked by cords of psychic energy that extend out from our heart. These cords are strongest to the people, animals and places to which we feel closest. In the unbounded dreamscape, information can travel more freely along these psychic lines.'

One characteristic that psychic dreams share is their strong emotional impact; the dreamer wakes with knowledge that the dream was highly important. Such dreams feel like a portent. The Chilean writer Isabel Allende uses her dreams to inspire her writing. She also dreamed the sex of her children before they were born and they already had names; it was clear to her that these names were not to be changed.

Dream recipients

Some people are able to tune in to psi communication. Like highly powered radio receivers, they pick up signals denied to less sensitive receivers. If you can accept that you may be able to tune into another layer of communication, either because it is an inherited characteristic or because it has not been driven underground by the negative views of others, you may regard your psychic dreams as extra-sensory gifts. Psi activity then happens more readily in your dreams, or nightly state of altered consciousness, because the waking censor in your mind does not immediately reject it.

Intuition often comes in the form of a flash of inspiration or a sudden understanding or awareness. This shows the sub-conscious mind cutting through the levels of conscious thinking to bring you to the heart of the matter. You may recognize it as the 'gut feeling' that informs you directly.

Psychic ability often runs in families. Shona told me, 'Both my son and I have psychic dreams. And my partner is used to me needing to be comforted after one of these. I see what is taking place through someone else's eyes, as if I am actually at the scene. I was a teenager when these dreams started and with age I've learnt to control them more.'

A dream that 'tells the future' can be disturbing, enlightening and life-affirming. If you experience this type of dream, it may help you to know that in more than thirty years of dream research talking to thousands of people about their dreams, and in my personal experience of such dreams, I have found psi dreams neither to be uncommon nor threatening.

Work with this exercise now Turn to Exercise 21: My Psi Profile on page 194 and follow the instructions.

I'm not there yet Don't worry if you're not yet ready to explore this form of dreaming. You might like to return to the Incubating My Dreams exercise on page 46.

Precognitive dreams

This is the term used to describe dreams that come before an event in our waking lives. They may be dreams that directly mirror that event, or dreams that prefigure events in a more symbolic way. In surveys reported by writer and dream researcher Anthony Shafton, between 25 and 50 per cent of Americans say they believe precognitive dreams; among African Americans, the figure is 92 per cent. He found that for African Americans the purpose of dreaming was to reveal future events and that ancestors were believed to speak through dreams. In the 19th century, Harriet Tubman, an African-American abolitionist born into slavery, had a dream about an underground railroad that offered slaves a route to escape from brutal captivity. She led hundreds to safety and said that her dreams helped her find safe routes so well that she did not lose a single 'passenger'.

Some dreams need to be read more symbolically. For example, the wife of the French King Henry IV had a dream before he was assassinated in 1610 that the gems on her crown had changed to pearls. Pearls were a symbol of mourning; it was not until after his death that she made the connection. The dream may have reflected her fears for his safety in the cut-throat world of royal politics at the time or it may have been a premonition of his death.

Some dreams are more explicit. In 1865, President of the United States Abraham Lincoln had a very detailed dream which he told many people because it was so shocking. In the dream he woke to hear sobbing in another room. Through the empty corridors he followed the sound to the East Room. 'There,' he said, 'I made a sickening surprise. Before me was a catafalque, on which rested a corpse.' He asked a soldier guarding the body who was dead in the White House. The reply was, 'The President. He was killed by an assassin.' It was the outpouring of grief from the mourners in his dream that woke President Lincoln. A few days later he was shot dead while visiting the theatre.

One of my clients, Nina, had an equally direct and explicit dream. 'I dreamed that a man I knew would have a fatal accident

on a particular stretch of road near his home. The dream was so intense that when he offered to give my friend and me a lift, I made up an excuse and refused. After he'd gone I told my friend about the dream.' Nina said, 'Can you imagine the horror I felt when this same girl rang me, a few days later, to tell me the dream had come true, down to the smallest detail.'

Time to prepare

Some dreams seem to warn or prepare us for a traumatic event that comes out of the blue. Such dreams come before an event takes place and suggest that although some events cannot be avoided they can be made less serious. Often they have an unusual quality which makes them stand out from your other dreams.

Sally had a dream that as she was waiting at traffic lights to turn into the road where her mother lived, a truck ran into the back of her car and shunted her into oncoming traffic. Her crushed car was so badly damaged that she had to be cut out of the wreckage. The day after the dream, she told colleagues at work, who jokily advised her not to drive for the rest of the week. Three days later the crash happened, in every detail, exactly as in her dream. When she came round in the intensive care unit, the first thing she remembered was the dream. Sally felt the dream had prepared her for the accident and knew she would recover. She has had other precognitive dreams set far in the future, which reassure her that she will live a long life, despite major health difficulties.

Maria's dream may have saved her life, too. 'I had a dream that I was driving down a dark, wet road and turned a corner. A car had broken down just around the bend and I crashed into it. Before I did so I noticed a 'Kent' sticker in the window and the registration number.' Some weeks later Maria was driving down a dark, wet road. As she was about to turn the corner she remembered the

dream. 'I slowed down enough to avoid the car with a Kent sticker and the same registration number as in my dream,' she said. 'I had told a friend about the dream and she was with me in the car.'

When there is a warning element in a dream it is wise not to ignore it. You might consider what you could change to avoid the situation or whether you could tell anyone else who featured in the dream.

Series of dreams

Angela had a recurring dream over many years. It started just after her 21st birthday. Unlike most of her other dreams, this dream was always in black and white. She told me:

'I am standing outside a church and graveyard. All is dark, the trees are bent by the force of the wind and the rain of a violent storm. The black sky is scarred by jagged lightning and the gravestones are set against the skyline. The violence of the storm and the deafening claps of thunder are terrifying. I stand outside the church gates holding a newborn infant in my arms, yet I am consumed by a dreadful sorrow, the like of which I had never experienced. I hold a baby, yet I mourn a baby. Always on waking from this dream the sorrow would persist.'

Angela married and had three children who also married. One night she dreamed about her pregnant daughter, and again the dream was in black and white.

'Toward the end of my daughter's pregnancy I dreamed that, at the dead of night, when the weather was stormy, I found her wandering in my uncultivated garden. She looked somewhat bewildered and her face was slightly swollen and spotted with blood. I asked what had happened and she told me that that the floor had opened beneath her and she had fallen through to the floor below. She then said, "But it is alright, the baby is not hurt."'

The dream filled Angela with foreboding. Her daughter died giving birth to the baby, her first child. After her death, Angela experienced a number of dreams in which her daughter was calling to her. She was shackled in a dark cellar and Angela could never release her. Months later Angela dreamed of her father who had died five years previously, her first dream of him since his death. In the dream she asked him how her daughter was and he told me that she was worried about me. 'I asked him if he had come for me and he walked rapidly away'. This dream was in colour.

Dreams that come in series reflect ongoing situations in our lives. Angela's dreams show her great disturbance after the traumatic death of her daughter and

185

her continued grief as she worked through her feelings of guilt because she had not saved her. Such reactions are frequently experienced by bereaved parents though, for Angela, there is an added dimension because she had these prophetic dreams. In the final dream, you can see that part of her wondered if it were her own turn to die – but this dream was in colour, unlike the others, so not prophetic. However, it is significant that the message of the dream is concern for Angela. It indicates that she needs to take care of herself, recognize that she could not have done more than she did, and somehow come to terms with her dreadful experience.

Work with this exercise now
Turn to Exercise 22: My Precognitive Self on page 198 and follow the instructions.

I'm not there yet Don't worry if you're not yet ready to explore this form of dreaming. You might like to return to the exercise incubating a healing dream on page 174.

Dream telepathy

Telepathy is the ability to communicate thoughts, feelings and desires without the use of ordinary means, such as speech, body language, phone or writing. This form of psychic communication can also take place in dreams and usually happens between people joined by bonds of blood or love. Psychoanalyst Sigmund Freud commented that 'sleep creates favourable conditions for telepathy' and described the telepathic dreams his patients told him.

The word *telepathy* derives from the Greek roots *tele*, meaning 'far' or 'distant', and *pathe*, meaning 'feeling'. The term was introduced in the 19th century by the English psychologist F.W. Myers, president of the Society for Psychical Research. In 1886, three of the society's founders published *Phantasms of the Living*, a study of the paranormal, and in it they quoted 149 examples of dream telepathy, which they claimed had been rigorously examined and verified. Many of my clients also report similar dreams.

In some cases, people share a psychic dream on the same night. If you are recording your dreams, you may recognize those that were telepathic and shared with others. It's useful to ask family or friends if they dream of you when you are dreaming of them. Often this confirms a telepathic link.

Megan told me of her telepathic dream: 'A friend was loading a dumper truck when it suddenly spilled and he was buried under the load. He had to be taken to hospital. I woke up screaming and two hours later my husband rang from work to tell me that this had actually happened, I was dreaming about it at the time it was happening.'

This is a telepathic dream because it happened at the same time as Megan's friend had the accident. There is an immediate link and Megan had not received the information through other channels but at the exact moment the event took place.

Telepathic dreams may prevent accidents from happening. An old family friend, Robin, had been staying with Lynn for the weekend. He left after

dinner and Lynn decided to go to bed. At 1.30am she woke screaming Robin's name and couldn't go back to sleep for worry about him. The next morning Robin rang her, saying, 'Thank you for waking me last night. You probably saved my life.' It seems he had fallen asleep while driving and at 1.30am had been woken by Lynn screaming at him.

Understanding telepathy

Research into quantum physics shows that atoms can be influenced to change their movements across the globe. Maybe as this research develops, we will finally have an explanation as to how

telepathy takes place. Until then, you can understand more about your own telepathic abilities by recording your dreams. Once you have amassed a good collection of dreams, each dated, you can look back and see if any were telepathic by comparing them with events that took place at the same time.

For some people, telepathy may feel quite frightening, but it can inform you of positive things or help you recognize that someone you care for needs help. The more you learn about your deeper, inner self, the more empowered you will feel to take control of your life.

 Work with this exercise now Turn to Exercise 23: Communicating in My Dreams on page 202 and follow the instructions.

Astral travel and out-of-body experiences

Dreaming is the time we can 'tune in' to our higher intelligence and, with practice, gain insight into our real selves and our purpose in life. Astral travel dreams and out-of-body experiences (OOBEs) are a useful tool for exploring this inner world.

During dreams of astral projection, the dreamer feels that she leaves her physical body and journeys to other places, visits the distant past or ventures into the future. As Leanne told me, 'I have experiences on the astral plane which can seem like dreams, but there is a difference. I have met my grandmother who has passed over and it was really wonderful to see her. At other times I leave my body and choose to go to see people or visit places I have not been to in my waking life.'

People who experience OOBEs frequently see themselves floating above their bodies and look at the reclining body below them. They speak of a feeling of freedom and lightness, which comes with being unencumbered by the physical body. The anthropologist Sir James Frazer, author of *The Golden Bough*, commented on an accepted belief in mythology from many belief systems that the soul can escape the body and visit the future as well as other realms.

Carol has been interested in psychic phenomena since a child, when she first experienced astral travel. She told me, 'In astral travel the spiritual, or subtle, body starts to detach itself from the feet upward until it is separated. In one dream I had my arms outstretched and was looking down over a vast landscape. I travelled to the edge of the Sea of Galilee and met a being who radiated brilliant light and knowledge.'

She awoke feeling renewed and full of joy. This was particularly important to her as she was going through a period of spiritual change and felt quite distressed. She added, 'Some dreams are like mystical experiences. Numerous times I feel I am leaving my body and feel very free and light. In this type of

dream I meet people and find myself in places I've never seen, although they frequently feel familiar It's in this sort of dream that I've seen future events.'

In my experience, such dreams are a great gift to the dreamer. They give another dimension to life and enable us to recognize that there are new dimensions to explore if we give ourselves permission to travel in places where there are no maps. We have to be courageous to make that journey.

Initiation dreams
Intuitive dreams often have a spiritual dimension that may help you to experience the divine, in whatever form that has meaning for you. Some people experience dreams of past lives or dreams that initiate them into new roles and worlds. Frequently these dreamers are on a spiritual quest and the dreams echo their waking practices. As it was for Julia. She told me, 'I began recording my dreams after I had the following dream: There is a small snake which looks like a cobra. It fitted on the thumb of a man. We were in a special room with some people I knew and others who were good friends though I did not know them in real life. Then the man pressed his thumb with the snake on it into my left eye. It hurt but I knew it was some

form of initiation.' When she woke, Julia felt this was an important dream, and it set her on the path of dream research.

In another dream a voice said, 'This is your first lesson.' Since then she has had many dreams in which she has been informed of what happens after death. In another, she says, 'I met a boy from India and dreamed that his mother was "keeper of the flame". There followed a complicated religious ceremony that did not make sense to him or me. His mother, whom I did not know, but was brought up as a Zoroastrian, recognized the ritual my dream described.'

Julia believed that the recognition of this ceremony conformed that she was being taught about a dimension she was previously unaware of. It enabled her to commit fully to her spiritual journey and reassured her that the path was right for her.

Exploring astral travel

Exploring astral travel and OOBEs in your own dreams may take time and practice, but you can start creating the right conditions by thinking about what you would like to do in an OOBE. Where would you go? Who would you visit? Because the possibilities are limitless, make sure you are motivated by the development of your higher, or more authentic, self. Spend some time meditating on the possibilities, and when you are ready, imagine that you are leaving your body but remain connected to it by a silken cord. This ensures that you can return to your physical body at any time.

 Work with this exercise now Turn to Exercise 24: My Astral Journey on page 206 and locate CD Track 6. Find a quiet place indoors where you can lie down comfortably, have a CD player nearby, then follow the instructions.

 I'm not there yet If you have difficulty thinking about out-of-body experiences, instead use the gentle relaxation exercise on page 16.

PSYCHIC DREAM EXERCISES

These exercises will help you explore the psychic dimension in your dreams, including communication with others in the dream state. They will help you deepen your experience of astral travel and out-of-body journeys.

Fitting the psi profile

You will need your dream diary for this exercise, which allows you to assess how closely your own dreams fit the profile of a psychic, or psi, dream. You are looking for indicators of telepathy, precognition, knowing of an event before it happens and unusual phenomena in your dreams.

 ## Exercise 21 MY PSI PROFILE
CD REFERENCE TRACK 1 (OPTIONAL)

When to do this exercise Whenever you would like to tune in to messages in your dreams. You will need to have recorded your dreams for some time.

- **Sit down with your dream diary** and refresh your memory by reading over dreams that appeal to you.

- **Look out for characteristics common to psi dreams.** These include dreams that feel highly realistic and have intense clarity. A dream may feel more like a 'felt' or sensory experience than a dream. The quality of light or colour is often different from regular dreams. You may also have a sense of being warned or prepared, and a guide or angelic being may speak to you. Make a note of any dreams that fit this description.

- **Now look back at dreams that fit these categories.** Can you can relate them to events that happened subsequently? To explore this further, answer the questions on page 195.

My psi profile experience

Questions to consider
How did I respond to any dreams that had psychic qualities?
How did I recognize the psychic element in the dream?
How did these dreams influence my actions?
What do I need to develop my higher self, or intuition?

Date _____ Time _____

_____

_____

_____

_____

_____

_____

Date _____ Time _____

_____

_____

_____

_____

_____

Date _____ Time _____

_____

_____

_____

_____

_____

_____

_____

_____

_____

Date _____ Time _____

_____

_____

_____

_____

_____

_____

_____

_____

_____

_____

Date _____ Time _____

_____

_____

_____

_____

_____

_____

_____

_____

Date _____ Time _____

_____

_____

_____

_____

_____

_____

_____

_____

Exploring precognitive dreams

This exercise is for the many people who have experienced a precognitive dream – one which seems to prepare you for or warn you about a future event. It also suits those who, when awake, have a sense that something is going to happen before it takes place. You will need your dream diary.

 ### Exercise 22 MY PRECOGNITIVE SELF
CD REFERENCE TRACK 1 (OPTIONAL)

When to do this exercise If you have had a precognitive dream (see pages 182–86) or a sense in your waking life that something is about to happen. You will need to have recorded your dreams for some time.

- **Look back at your dream diary.** Can you spot any dreams or remember any waking events that could be described as a precognitive experience?

- **List your dreams and experiences** and make a note of how you felt at the time each one happened.

- **Now think back to how you reacted** – and the impact on your life and relationships when the foretold event happened. Use these notes to answer the questions on page 199.

My precognitive self experience

Questions to consider

How do I feel now as I look at my list of precognitive experiences?
Would I like to develop this ability?
In what ways might I do this?
Have I any fears that I need to explore?
Could I share these experiences with members of my family, who may also
have precognitive experiences?

Date _____ Time _____

_____

_____

_____

_____

_____

Date _____ Time _____

_____

_____

_____

_____

_____

Date _____ Time _____

_____

_____

_____

_____

_____

_____

_____

_____

_____

Date _____ Time _____

_____

_____

_____

_____

_____

_____

_____

_____

_____

Date _____ Time _____

_____
_____
_____
_____
_____
_____
_____
_____

Date _____ Time _____

_____
_____
_____
_____
_____
_____
_____
_____

Exploring your telepathic skills

You already have experiences of communicating with others in your dreams – when you talk with friends or family, meet a loved one who has died or see an old school friend and exchange news. Sometimes, a friend will tell you that they dreamed about you on the night you dreamed of them. This exercise helps you to explore these thoughts.

 Exercise 23 COMMUNICATING IN MY DREAMS
CD REFERENCE TRACK 1 (OPTIONAL)

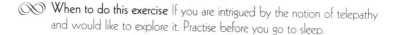 **When to do this exercise** If you are intrigued by the notion of telepathy and would like to explore it. Practise before you go to sleep.

- **Before you go to sleep** think of someone you would like to communicate with telepathically tonight.

- **Now visualize yourself** in the dream realm spending time with that person.

- **While you spend time with that person** in your imagination, rehearse what you would like to talk about.

- **Let yourself fall asleep** and in the morning record your dream. You might like to share it with the person you wanted to communicate with.

- **Consider** the questions on page 203.

My dream communication experience

Questions to consider
Who did I choose to communicate with?
What did I want from that encounter?
What did I discover as I explored my telepathic skills?
What conditions would enhance my telepathic skills?

Date _____ Time _____

_____
_____
_____
_____
_____
_____

Date _____ Time _____

_____
_____
_____
_____
_____

Date _____ Time _____

_____

_____

_____

_____

_____

_____

_____

_____

_____

Date _____ Time _____

_____

_____

_____

_____

_____

_____

_____

_____

_____

Date _____ Time _____

_____

_____

_____

_____

_____

_____

_____

_____

_____

Date _____ Time _____

_____

_____

_____

_____

_____

_____

_____

_____

Exploring out-of-body experiences

This journey out of your physical body starts with a gentle relaxation before guiding you safely through an out-of-body visualization. Find a quiet, warm place to practise where you won't be disturbed.

 Exercise 24 MY ASTRAL JOURNEY
CD REFERENCE TRACK 6 (TO FOLLOW THE SCRIPT, TURN TO PAGE 248)

When to do this exercise If you would like to start creating the right conditions for an out-of-body experience. You should be motivated by the development of your higher self.

- **Lie down comfortably** and allow your body to fully relax.

- **Read the text** on pages 248–49 and when ready turn on Track 6 and follow the guided meditation.

- **When you have finished,** consider the questions on page 207.

My astral journey experience

Questions to consider
How did I feel when I was out of my body?
What did I see from this different viewpoint?
Where did I visit and how did it feel?
What else have I brought back from this experience?

Date _____ Time _____

_____

_____

_____

_____

_____

_____

Date _____ Time _____

_____

_____

_____

_____

_____

_____

Date _____ Time _____

_____

_____

_____

_____

_____

_____

_____

_____

_____

Date _____ Time _____

_____

_____

_____

_____

_____

_____

_____

_____

_____

_____

TAKING DREAMWORK FURTHER

Developing dream wisdom

Dreams can be portholes into the future – as the ancient Greeks regarded them – or portholes into the past – the view held by psychoanalyst Sigmund Freud. Now you have worked on many aspects of your dreaming self, it is time to progress to more advanced dreamwork, to deepen the insight into your past and future offered by your dreams. As you work through this section of the book and over time you will develop a directory of symbols unique to you. You will also learn to re-enter your dreams in a waking meditative state, bringing you closer to your higher self and helping to

integrate it into your everyday self. Psychotherapist Carl Jung named this process of coming to better understand the self as 'the individuation process'. Such inner growth is frequently expressed in an extended series of dreams. When you look back on them, you will see developments that may not have been obvious at the time.

Gaining in understanding

The Italian writer and painter Carlo Levi said, '*Il futuro ha un cuore antico*': the future has an ancient heart. Events that happen today may have been seeded years before. You may find evidence of present actions being laid down in earlier dreams as you look back at your dream record.

Kimberley is a survivor of sexual abuse and trained as a psychotherapist. Throughout her recovery, she kept a record of her dreams. She says, 'I have kept a dream journal for over fifteen years and notice how they have changed as my own healing process took place. My dreams have given me the ability to understand what was going on at times when I was confused and lost. They were

an important guide. My most powerful dreams have come before transitional points in my life and have included a male figure who is old and wise and has the status of a guide. In some ways my active dream life has also been a source of vibrancy and life when I have been paralyzed with fear in my waking life.'

Advanced techniques

As you are now well practised in recording and interpreting your dreams, it's time to introduce more advanced techniques that extend the ways in which you respond to your dreams and allow you to learn even more from your dreaming self. This stretches you, shifting you out of your comfort zone into a newer, more profound area of learning. Try the following ways of responding creatively to your dreams:

Express your dream visually Use paint, crayons or marbling inks to produce a mood painting rather than a realistic representation of the contents of the dream. Or you could make a mandala (see page 226).

Use natural objects Recreate the dream in 3D, using clay, feathers, leaves and seed heads and making marks with stones. This helps to connect the natural world with your dream world.

Think musically Find a piece of music that expresses your dream. Listen to it and contemplate the ways in which the music extends your understanding of your dream.

Use physical gesture Express your dream in movement or dance. You might imagine you are one of the characters in the dream and move like him or her. Exaggerate the movements to make them more dramatic. How does it feel? What do you learn?

Research the subject If you dream about certain animals learn more about them. What part of the world do they live in? What relationships do they have with humans? Collect pictures, draw the animal or make a collage. All these responses honour the dream and deepen your creative link to it.

 Work with this exercise now Turn to Exercise 25: My Dream Mandala on page 226 and follow the instructions.

Your personal symbol directory

While recording your dreams as you worked through the book, you may have noticed certain symbols appearing regularly: particular people, places, animals, objects and so on. To better appreciate and learn from these symbols, create your own dream-symbol directory. You can do this over a period of weeks, years or even over a lifetime. Start with a card index, a loose-leafed file or a computer file, and record the name of the symbol on a new card or page, accompanied by a short description. On the back of the card or on another page, write your personal associations to the symbol. Include feelings, the memories it evokes and how it connects to your work, culture or faith. Also make connections to word play and puns.

You may find that over time your dream symbols change. As you develop your inner wisdom, so your symbols will reflect that change. Paula first dreamed of a lioness when she was having problems settling into a new

job. In her dreams the lioness was prowling in a threatening way and looking at her. As she became more confident and successful at work she

dreamed that the lioness approached her and lay down beside her, purring contentedly.

To gain most benefit from working with symbols, it is helpful to cultivate the art of thinking in images. The explanations on the following pages will help you to start thinking in this way. Use your intuitive awareness and creativity to help you harvest the rich symbolic material from the unconscious. Symbols and images come from the teeming, unseen world of primal creativity into your waking world, where you can activate them in whatever creative form seems most appropriate.

Many of the symbols that appear in dreams are a channel through which higher aspects of yourself can emerge. As these aspects become part of your waking life, you will find that you benefit from their 'compressed' energy, which helps to 'open up' your spiritual qualities as well as your intuition, inspiration and wisdom. To access these qualities in your waking hours, you can meditate on particularly intense, beautiful or vivid symbols in your dreams – these often take the form of natural objects. When you meditate on a symbol, the energy in the symbol is released and becomes available to you; you assimilate the power of the symbol.

Reading common symbols

On the following pages you will find some common associations of symbols often found in dreams. This will help you to reflect on what certain motifs mean for you. As with all elements of dreams, your waking life and relationships will inform each symbol's personal meaning. Dreaming of horses, for example, will mean different things to a jockey or dressage competitor than to someone frightened of horses.

Animal symbols

Like humans, animals are born, mate and die, and they sometimes have attributes that seem all-too human. This is reflected in their appearance in myths, fables, folk tales and children's stories. The Pied Piper pipes away the infestation of rats, then pipes away the children of the town when his fee is not paid. The Ugly Duckling undergoes a transformation to become his beautiful self. In *The Jungle Book*, a host of animals display their individuality. Such stories become part of our language and we bring the strengths and weaknesses of their characters into our personal dream symbology.

Typically, horses symbolize wild, animal passion and strength. Birds and other creatures with wings are portrayed across cultures as messengers to other worlds and the world of dreams and visions. In initiation ceremonies, bird feathers form part of masks and headdresses. For the wearer of a headdress or crown, this symbolizes direct contact with heaven and the gods, which is why they are so important in shamanistic ceremonies.

Body symbols

Many of our waking and dreaming metaphors and symbols relate to the body, its organs and functions. Some examples that regularly occur are birth, symbolized as a person emerging from water, by a sea or lake or emerging from a dark cave. Babies in dreams often represent actual new births or new beginnings. A baby may stand for the dreamer at the start of a new venture, discovering new skills and talents, or the beginning of a new creative process.

For the ancient Greeks, a dream in which the planets were orbiting the sun in the wrong order or were out of their customary orbit, signified a disturbance in the dreamer's body.

Some erotic dreams may have explicit body and sexual imagery, including sexual relationships with the same or opposite sex, with family members or work colleagues, or with beings and creatures that are completely alien to the dreamer. These dreams can be shocking or arousing. The energy in dreams of a sexual nature relates to creativity and fertility. One study found that creative students had more unconventional erotic dreams than their less creative colleagues. Dreams can give you ideas that may increase your sexual satisfaction, too. As Paulette says, 'My dreams are an outlet for my fantasies. In some I have sex with people I don't know, wear sexy underwear, have homosexual encounters – all of which I don't do in my waking life. The dreams seem to make up for that.'

Clothing symbols

Clothes represent the persona we show to the world: the well-groomed business woman, the rebellious anarchist, the country gent or the devout Muslim. The clothes we choose carry information about how we would like to be seen and treated. Clothing also symbolizes status and rank. A queen may be entitled to wear a crown, so if you are not from a royal household and find yourself wearing a crown in your

dreams, it may indicate a desire for greater status. In your dreams you may be searching for the perfect outfit, dressing up or finding yourself out in public dressed only in a short vest. We sometimes have an ambiguous relationship with our clothes, using them to cover our nakedness and yet also to draw attention to ourselves.

Food symbols

In dreams, food can reveal our attitudes to what we eat and symbolize how we feel about receiving, ingesting and eliminating it once we have extracted all

the goodness we can. Food in dreams may also be linked to other appetites: sexual, desire for success or recognition and spiritual needs.

When you dream of food, are you eating or feeding others? Are you the nurturer or the nurtured? Is food a source of comfort and consolation, perhaps symbolizing a time when you could rely on others to nurture you, such as in childhood? Preparing and serving food represents taking care of others and may indicate a 'mothering' role.

House symbols

The house in a dream may represent your current home or a house you have lived in in the past. However, dream houses often symbolize the dreamer's body and mind. You can see the similarities: like our bodies, houses have openings and passages; they have windows that let in light as our eyes do, and we take food into houses as we take food into our own bodies. We also have to eliminate that food, and houses have bathrooms and pipes to take away the waste just as we have our own waste-disposal system. Houses have different floors with different functions, though connected by doors, staircases and corridors. The head, at the top of the body is often symbolized by an attic. One of my clients told me, 'When I dream of doors, they represent decisions or choices. When I see a door I can decide to enter or stay outside. I dreamed of a huge hall with dozens of black doors. I feel I always have a multitude of choices, hence the multitude of doors. The dream starts in my place of birth because my brain takes me there to solve problems'.

Many people dream about toilets. Sometimes they are unusable, dirty and overflowing; in other cases the dreamer is searching in vain for one she can use. In one of Ami's recurring dreams she is desperate to use the toilet but the ones she finds all lack doors, making her visible to anyone passing. The dreams are set in all sorts of places, but none Ami is familiar with in her waking life. This type of dream may reveal feelings of being vulnerable, of being unable to complete things, of being exposed or unable to eliminate waste.

Travel symbols

Life is often described as a journey. The main journey is from birth to death; in between may be destinations we choose to set out for or detours that take us to unknown territory. Travel dreams with setbacks, missed flights, crossed communications or other obstacles may symbolize missed opportunities. Journeys underground may relate to feelings of being in the dark. We may need to explore the darkness in order to shed light on hidden knowledge.

A traveller usually has luggage, tickets, bags and personal requirements for the journey. Dream luggage may symbolize unfinished business that you carry with you wherever you go – perhaps burdens, responsibilities and obligations. If dream luggage seems to be weighing you down, how could you travel more lightly on an emotional level?

Vehicle symbols

Cars and other vehicles are capable of great power and speed and have the ability to transport us from place to place. They usually protect the driver and passengers from the elements and can be a status symbol. Dream cars often symbolize the physical state of the dreamer. Difficulties with steering may indicate anxiety about being in control. Concerns about running out of fuel, the fuel not being suitable for that make of car or about putting in the wrong fuel may relate to lack of energy or resources.

If you dream of a car, think about it in detail. Is this a high-performance model or a wreck? Is it well maintained? Do the brakes work? How about the driver: can she control the car or is it difficult to drive? The answers to such questions help you understand how the dream car symbolizes aspects of your life. The driver of the car has symbolic importance. If you, the dreamer, are driving the car, it indicates a level of control, but the way you drive, your level of confidence and your reactions to other drivers all convey information, too. If someone else is driving your car, has that person taken over your life in some way? You may also dream of back-seat drivers who interfere with your progress or of a helpful map reader who navigates for you.

One of my clients, Caiti, dreamed that the brakes on her car failed as she was speeding down a motorway on the wrong side of the carriageway. The lights of the oncoming cars nearly blinded her and before a terrible crash happened, she woke. After thinking about the different elements of her dream she recognized that she was going in the wrong direction in life and not seeing what was truly happening. She needed to put on the brakes to stop her present behaviour. The dream woke her to the danger she was in at a turbulent time in her life.

Shape symbols

If images of geometric shapes or objects fill your dreams, meditate on them to understand their significance. The circle is a recurring symbol found in dreams. It signifies wholeness, completion and eternity. The mandala image (see pages 226–29) is also associated with the self, and *mandala* is a Sanskrit word, meaning 'disc', 'circle' or 'magic circle'.

 Work with this exercise now Turn to Exercise 26: My Dream Wisdom on page 230 and locate CD Track 7. Find a quiet place indoors where you can sit or lie down comfortably, have a CD player nearby and follow the instructions.

 I'm not there yet You might like to refresh yourself on universal dream themes by working through Exercise 12 on page 110.

Lucid dreaming

During lucid dreaming, a dreamer is aware that she is dreaming and can exert some control over what happens in the dream. In this way, lucid dreaming holds open the door between the conscious self and the unconscious mind.

The term was coined by Dutch psychiatrist Frederik Van Eeden in 1913. Van Eeden presented a paper to the British Society for Psychical Research in which he described the nature of 350 of his lucid dreams, collected over a period of 14 years. Lucid dreaming was not a new phenomenon then. In 1867, the French scientist, le Marquis d'Hervey-Saint-Denys, published *Dreams and the Ways to Direct Them; Practical Observations*, which focused on dream control. And many spiritual leaders have always practised lucid dreaming. In 12th-century Tibet, schools of Dream Masters used lucid dreams as a form of meditation to enhance the process of enlightenment. In the early 20th century, Georges Gurdjieff, an Armenian charismatic mystic, and P.D. Ouspensky, his disciple, used lucid dreams to deepen their spiritual knowledge.

The 'lucid' part of the description refers to the clarity of consciousness in these kinds of dreams, rather than the vividness of the dream. The intensity of a lucid dream can be almost beyond words. Occult writer Oliver Fox, writing of his first lucid dream at 16 years of age, expressed his amazement both at the vividness of his surroundings and the exquisite freedom and clear-headedness he felt for an instant.

The history of lucid dreaming

Animistic shamanism is probably the earliest of spiritual vocations. Shamans were often chosen because of their ability to dream lucidly. In their lucid dreams they travelled between dimensions in which other spirits and powers reign, and from the daytime world of wakefulness to the world of dreaming. The sense of freedom this gives is recorded on Indigenous Australian bark paintings from the 19th century, which show shamans depicting themselves with wings or as birds. Sometimes shamans are said to speak the language of the birds or 'the tongue of secret wisdom', codes known only to the initiated.

All shamanistic traditions rely on dreams for information and warnings. A shaman may journey between three worlds – the middle world, upper world and lower world – to access divination and healing. In these inner journeys the shaman may be guided by a power animal (see pages 90–91) or transformed into another creature in order to access its characteristics and strengths.

In Native American cultures, children who are born with natural psychic, or shamanistic, talents are supposed to 'walk with them', not reject them. The dangers of not learning to live with them are regarded as mental illness. Schizophrenia is explained as the inability to know which inner voices to listen to and which to ignore.

The Minangkabau people of West Sumatra province, Indonesia, have a belief that the *sumanghat*, or true life-force, leaves the body in dreams and when a person is seriously ill. Like the shamans of Siberia, these travellers between realms must bring back cures for the sick and disperse evil spirits who may harm supplicants seeking aid from the shaman. In lucid dreams shamans also guide the dead to their new abode, where they are reunited with ancestors who have gone before them.

Understanding the phenomenon

Dr Stephen LaBerge, a psychologist who founded The Lucidity Institute in Palo Alto, California, has made invaluable contributions to our understanding of lucid dreaming and the ways in which we can use it for self-development. He has found that although only 5–10 per cent of people are natural lucid dreamers, many of us can learn to develop lucid-dreaming skills. In many instances, dreams of flying are precursors of lucid dreaming. The element of control over where to fly, the style of flying with arms outstretched, like playing planes as a child, and the quality of the experience have much in common with lucid dreaming As Gian told me, 'When I was a child I often used to dream of flying. I flew reluctantly at first, then I got frightened because I flew higher and higher and could not come down.' As an adult, her dreams have changed but still involve flight: 'In some dreams I resemble a hummingbird because I can hover in one spot. I can look in on second storey windows. It's a thrilling phenomenon.'

You may become aware of being in a dream as you sleep and can say to yourself, 'I am dreaming and I can continue this dream'. This is the first indicator of lucid dreaming.

 Work with this exercise now Turn to Exercise 27: My Lucid Dream on page 234 and follow the instructions.

 I'm not there yet Being able to dream lucidly may not happen right away, but try not to give up on yourself or the practice. Have confidence that, with practice and in time, you will be able to experience this great gift.

The uses of lucid dreams

Anxiety dreams and nightmares can be overcome through lucid dreaming, because if you know you are dreaming, you have nothing to fear: dream images cannot hurt you. Moreover, in lucid dreaming you lead your dreams to satisfying conclusions. You can face your frightening characters and change them or adapt events to give you greater mastery.

Like many lucid dreamers, John met his dream guide in a dream. He told me, 'Lucid dreaming has been a bonus. With the controls and options I have, I can focus my attention on the "dis-ease" in my life and try to help others through my insights. On many occasions I have been able to "send light" from my lucid dream vantage point.' Because of his experiences of lucid dreaming, John feels more confident, has greater understanding of others and more profound insight into his past lives. 'I have learned that life itself is relative and not absolute. We need integration and growth on all levels and that, of course, means in our dream lives, too.'

Learning to dream lucidly

In order to create the best possible circumstances for lucid dreams, try these simple techniques before you go to sleep:

Review your day Think back through your day to clear the clutter from your mind, celebrate the positives and consider how you can change negative behaviour or unhelpful thoughts. This helps to keep you strong spiritually. Start with where you are now – lying in bed – and simply wind the clock back to when you woke up. Recall both the positives and the negatives of the day, ensuring you create a balance between the two. Consider how you've acted during the day and what was important to you.

Recognize your dream state While you are dreaming, ask yourself, 'Am I dreaming?' In your mind's eye, look at your hands and feet. Are they their normal size? If they are different, you are probably dreaming. Try to do something that might be difficult or impossible in waking life – try to fly, perhaps, or somersault as if you were weightless. If you can do these actions, you are having a lucid dream.

Remind yourself During your dream, keep reminding yourself that you are indeed dreaming.

◈◈ **Work with this exercise now** Turn to Exercise 28: Becoming More Whole on page 238, then follow the instructions.

EXERCISES TO EXTEND YOUR DREAMWORK

These exercises will add depth to all the dreamwork you have done so far and help to develop mindfulness, or being in the moment, as you create a mandala. They also celebrate the wonderful gifts and guides your dreams can bring and the power of lucid dreaming.

Making a mandala

Tibetan monks a create mandalas from sand as part of a deep meditative practice. These geometric patterns, used to focus the mind, often comprise a central motif surrounded by balanced patterns. The shape and contents have a sense of wholeness. To create your own mandala you will need a piece of graph or grid paper, coloured pencils, a ruler and a compass or circular template about 15 cm (6 in) across (a bowl or plate will do). You will also need your dream diary.

 Exercise 25 MY DREAM MANDALA
CD REFERENCE TRACK 1 (OPTIONAL)

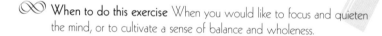 **When to do this exercise** When you would like to focus and quieten the mind, or to cultivate a sense of balance and wholeness.

- **Draw a circle** on the graph paper, using the compass or circular template.

- **Within the circle**, use the ruler to draw lines that dissect the circle. Alternatively, use the compass or circular template to draw curved lines that intersect the circle. Continue to divide the circle in this way until you have created a pattern that satisfies you.

- **Now choose colours** to fill in the shapes you have made. As you colour in, focus your attention on the act of colouring, as a form of meditation. Whenever your mind drifts to other thoughts, bring it back to the colouring. Trust the process; the aim is not to create a perfect mandala, but to allow yourself to create a symbol of completeness.

- **When the mandala is complete**, spend time looking at it. Try to immerse yourself in its colours and designs. Then write down how you felt about the process and what you feel about the mandala you have created, using the questions on page 227.

My dream mandala experience

Questions to consider
How has making the mandala contributed to my sense of well-being?
Are there any connections between the mandala I made and my dream symbols?
Where can I place this mandala so that I honour the creation process?

Date _____ Time _____

_____

_____

_____

_____

_____

_____

Date _____ Time _____

_____

_____

_____

_____

_____

_____

Date _____ Time _____

_____

_____

_____

_____

_____

_____

_____

_____

_____

Date _____ Time _____

_____

_____

_____

_____

_____

_____

_____

_____

_____

Date _____ Time _____

_____

_____

_____

_____

_____

_____

_____

_____

Date _____ Time _____

_____

_____

_____

_____

_____

_____

_____

_____

Dream gifts

In this exercise you try to identify the gifts given to you in dream form, and the guides who have imparted that wisdom – wisdom that has allowed you to grow and flourish. Choose a warm place to practise, where you will not be disturbed. As you consider the gifts your dreams have brought, thank your inner spirit that has allowed them to manifest.

Exercise 26 MY DREAM WISDOM

CD REFERENCE TRACK 7 (TO FOLLOW THE SCRIPT, TURN TO PAGE 249)

When to do this exercise First practise the relaxation exercise on page 16 to prepare your mind and body for this experience.

- **Lie down** comfortably and relax completely.
- **Read the text** on pages 249–50 and when ready turn on Track 7 and follow the guided meditation.
- **When you have finished,** consider the questions on page 231.

My dream wisdom experience

Questions to consider
What figures have come to me again and again through my dreams?
Which gifts from my dreams have assisted my emotional development?
Which gifts from my dreams have assisted my physical development?
Which gifts from my dreams have assisted my spiritual development?

Date _____ Time _____

_____

_____

_____

_____

_____

Date _____ Time _____

_____

_____

_____

_____

_____

Date _____ Time _____

_____

_____

_____

_____

_____

_____

_____

_____

_____

Date _____ Time _____

_____

_____

_____

_____

_____

_____

_____

_____

_____

Date _____ Time _____

_____

_____

_____

_____

_____

_____

_____

_____

_____

Date _____ Time _____

_____

_____

_____

_____

_____

_____

_____

_____

_____

Lucid dreaming

It can take years of working with your dreams to be able to dream lucidly, so don't worry if you only remember a snatched fragment at first. With practice, your skills should increase. Enjoy the sensation of flying and travelling in dreams which may be precursors to lucid dreaming.

 Exercise 27 MY LUCID DREAM
CD REFERENCE TRACK 1 (OPTIONAL)

 **When to do this exercise** While lying in bed, before you go to sleep. If it helps, practise the relaxation exercise on page 16 before you start.

- **Lie in bed**, making yourself comfortable, and fully relax. Repeat the following words to yourself, either out loud or silently: 'Tonight, my dream will be lucid.'

- **Repeat the words** to yourself a number of times, until they are firmly fixed in your mind.

- **Now as you drift toward sleep,** keep the positive words, or affirmation, in mind.

- **When you wake,** note how much lucidity you experienced in your dreams. To jog your memory, ask yourself the questions on page 235.

My lucid dream experience

Questions to consider

How much lucidity did I experience in my dream?
What was different about this dream to other dreams I have had?
What did I particularly enjoy about this experience?

Date _____ Time _____

_____

_____

_____

_____

_____

_____

_____

Date _____ Time _____

_____

_____

_____

_____

_____

_____

_____

Date _____ Time _____

_____

_____

_____

_____

_____

_____

_____

_____

_____

Date _____ Time _____

_____

_____

_____

_____

_____

_____

_____

_____

_____

_____

Date _____ Time _____

_____

_____

_____

_____

_____

_____

_____

_____

_____

Date _____ Time _____

_____

_____

_____

_____

_____

_____

_____

_____

_____

Wholeness and integration

In the final dreamwork technique in the book, you look back over your work to determine how far you have come. You will see how you have transformed the way you think and behave, noticing the effect your dream life has had on your waking hours. You will need your dream diary.

 ## Exercise 28 BECOMING MORE WHOLE
CD REFERENCE TRACK 1 (OPTIONAL)

When to do this exercise This is a very important exercise, so only attempt it after working through the book. Give yourself plenty of time — as much as two hours would be good and even longer if you have the time.

- **Find a lengthy series of dreams in your journal** and read through your notes. Think about the associations that arise with these dreams.

- **Consider any archetypes** and heroic figures (see pages 84–87) and any guides (see page 64) who have appeared to you. Make a note of how they have changed or developed over time.

- **Now look** for any movement toward wholeness or integration in these dreams. If this is not obvious, it may help to ask yourself the questions on page 239.

My wholeness experience

Questions to consider

Can I see how different elements have contributed to my personal development?
How have archetypes such as the Shadow emerged?
How have the qualities of the archetype become more integrated into my waking life?
Have any other archetypes accompanied me on my journey?

Date _____ Time _____

_____

_____

_____

_____

_____

Date _____ Time _____

_____

_____

_____

_____

_____

Date _____ Time _____

_____

_____

_____

_____

_____

_____

_____

_____

_____

Date _____ Time _____

_____

_____

_____

_____

_____

_____

_____

_____

_____

INSPIRATIONS

You will find these visualization exercises on the CD that accompanies this book. Use them as directed in the exercises, or let them inspire your own dreamwork.

Meeting My Guide

THIS TRACK EXPLORES THE POSSIBILITY OF MEETING A DREAM GUIDE
IN A VISUALIZATION.

- **Now that you are relaxed and prepared**, you are ready to meet your Higher Self, your spirit guide, your totem animal or any other aspect of spirit energy. Try to decide what form of your spirit energy you would like to meet. Take your time as you make your choice.

- **With the whole of your being**, think about how this encounter might change your life. What would it bring to your health and well-being? Consider all the opportunities such a meeting might bring.

- **Let your mind widen to visualize the perfect place** to have an encounter with your spirit guide. Imagine yourself walking around this setting. Smell its scents. Feel the air on your skin. Focus your intention on what you would like to gain from this experience and repeat the following words to yourself, 'I wish to meet my spirit guide'. Gently repeat the words. Feel them in your heart as you sincerely state your request one more time.

- **Visualize a path** that will take you to this perfect meeting place. See yourself travelling there in whatever form feels best. Take your time; this coming together is worth treasuring and need not be rushed.

- **Allow yourself to meet your spirit guide.**

- **What do you see before you?** Let your eyes travel over the vision, the spirit energy, taking note of the form, colours, textures and any intriguing details that claim your attention. Is there any aroma that accompanies the vision? Listen carefully for any sounds that are present. Use all your senses to fix this spirit energy in your memory.

- **How do you feel** now that you have met this powerful being? Be aware of any sensations in your body. Notice how you feel and the strength of your emotions.

- **As you feel bathed in the warming glow** of its presence, perhaps you could make a request or ask for help with a particular concern. Do this now.

- **You may hear a response to your request.** Listen carefully and keep it in your memory so that you can reflect on it later.

- **When you are ready,** take your leave and thank the spirit guide or totem animal for meeting you.

- **Know that now you have had this meeting,** you can revisit this safe place whenever you want to. The spirit connection has been made and will be with you whenever you want or need it.

- **Bring your attention back to the room.** Ground yourself in the here and now, feeling the sensation of your body on the surface on which it lies. Feel it supported by the bed or mat that you are lying on. Gently, re-enter your waking world

CD TRACK 3
Re-Entering My Dreams

THIS TRACK DETAILS HOW TO USE GUIDED IMAGERY TO CARRY ON A DREAM
IN A CONTROLLED WAY FROM THE POINT WHERE IT ENDED.

- **Allow yourself to recall a dream that you had recently.** Whatever the content of the dream, you are now in control and can stop the dream at any point.

- **Imagine yourself back in the dream** and guide yourself through the dream as if in slow motion so that you can appreciate each detail. Take all the time you need to immerse yourself fully in the dream.

- **Visualize yourself returning to the last part of the dream.** Carefully observe the people in the dream at this ending point. Note the setting and any particularly striking elements. Let your breathing become deeper as you see yourself back in the dream.

- **Now choose to re-enter the dream**, picking it up at the point it ended and continuing the story. If you were not at ease or unhappy about how the dream was developing, change the tone so it becomes more positive. You are in control; however you want to change the dream, go ahead and do it.

- **Think about how you want the dream to continue.** Give yourself permission to take it forward. Give yourself time to play the dream forward as you decide how it is to develop. Concentrate on that now.

- **Let yourself explore** the meaning of the way you imagined your dream continuing. How did you feel about what happened?

- **Was there anything that surprised you?**

- **Was there anything significant** that you did that you feel good about?

- **What is the message** that comes from the further development of the dream?

- **Celebrate your ability to take control** in your dream re-entry. What positive words can you say to yourself at this point?

- **Re-state those positive words.**

- **Now bring your attention back to the room** in which you are sitting. Be aware of the ground beneath you. When you are ready, open your eyes to your waking world. Celebrate your ability to take control of your dream re-entry.

CD TRACK 4
My Creative Release

THIS TRACK USES A CRYSTAL TO HELP UNBLOCK YOUR CREATIVE ENERGY.

- **For this visualization you need a cleansed crystal.** Choose one that really feels important to you today. Once you have reached a state of calm relaxation, lie down in a comfortable, safe space with your cleansed crystal in your left hand.

- **Focus your attention on the crystal.** Be aware of how it feels in your hand. Notice the colour. See how the light reflects from its surface. Bathe yourself in the light and colours.

- **Be aware** of any physical or emotional sensations that are happening now.

- **Allow yourself to reflect** on the creativity your crystal brings to your life. Place all your attention on the aspect of creativity you desire right now.

- **Think about** how the qualities of this crystal bring positive energy into your life. Still holding the crystal in your hand, visualize yourself in your bed sleeping soundly and serenely.

- **Visualize soothing blue, healing light** encircling your bed and yourself. See the protective light filling with dreams that bring you creative fulfilment.

- **Picture your crystal** lying beneath your pillow radiating its creative light into your dreaming self.

- **As you lie in this warming light,** make your request for enhanced creativity in whatever form you wish it to be. What do you need in your creative life right now? What can your higher self, your spirit guides and your crystal bring you now that will add to your sense of wholeness and well-being.

- **Visualize yourself communicating this to your crystal.** What words do you use? Repeat them out loud. This is to programme your crystal, to fill it with your request so it can help you in whatever way you have requested. With the power of the crystal your creativity is strengthened.

- **Now that you have programmed your crystal** with your request, picture it surrounded by an intense white light. This light holds the purity of your intention and affirms the power of the crystal to aid you in your dream journeys. Concentrate on that powerful white light.

- **Bring your attention back** to where you are in your comfortable safe space. Feel your body supported by the bed or mat that you are lying on. Feel the creative energy that your crystal holds for you.

- **Thank your crystal** for the power it brings to your creative self. Tonight, when you go to bed, place the crystal under your pillow and request a dream that will enhance your creativity.

CD TRACK 5
My Healing Visualization

THIS TRACK RELAXES YOU AND HELPS YOUR DREAMS TO GUIDE YOU BACK INTO A STATE OF BALANCE AND WHOLENESS.

- **Relax every part of your body.** Once your breathing has become calm and steady, with your next breath imagine you are lying on a yellow velvet couch. It is soft and luxuriant. You feel a gentle heat rising into your back. Notice the glow of vital healing energy circulating through your body. Be aware of this warmth, which allows your body to relax and repair itself.

- **Imagine you are surrounded by a yellow aura.** Yellow is the colour of your solar plexus chakra and holds most light. Let the light that radiates through your body release all your negative thoughts and feelings. Imagine the golden yellow light dissolving all the stresses that bring you discomfort just as sunlight dissolves early-morning mist.

- **Feel yourself supported and enfolded** by the grace of this healing light. If you wish, you may make a request now for specific healing, perhaps because a dream has alerted you to an area of concern. In the warm security of this visualization, ask for something that will help you, both now and in the future.

- **Now allow your thoughts to soften** and consider the ancient alchemists who sought to distil impurities in order to transform base metal into gold. They called this the 'great work'.

- **Think about how you, too, have been striving** through your life to become the highest form of being you can be. Early in life you may have prioritized worldly, material and financial achievements. Think of these now.

- **Consider a point in your life** when you decided to purify your inner base metal and uncover your inner wholeness. Was this prompted by trauma or illness, or perhaps spiritual or philosophical contemplation? Think about whether symbols of transformation appeared in you dreams. What do you feel you need to work on to discover your inner 'gold'?

- **What changes have taken place** in your inner world as you journey to completeness? Think deeply about what you have achieved and congratulate yourself on overcoming some obstacles that have blocked your path.

- **Take time to thank your inner guides** that have taken you on this alchemical path which has brought you to where you are to day. Finally, repeat this affirmation, saying to yourself, 'I will continue the journey to find my highest self, emotionally, physically and spiritually.'

- **Now, gently bring your attention back to your body.** Feel it supported by the bed or mat that you are lying on. When you are ready, open your eyes and slowly look around at your surroundings as you experience the deep relaxation that fills you.

CD TRACK 6
My Astral Journey

THIS TRACK GUIDES YOU SAFELY THROUGH AN OUT-OF-BODY VISUALIZATION

- **As you lie in your comfortable space,** observe your breath flowing in and out of your nostrils until your breathing is regular and you feel in harmony with the world.

- **Gently focus your attention on your body.** Visualize yourself lying exactly where you are in this room. Feel the bed or mat beneath your relaxed physical body.

- **Now it is time to turn your attention to your inner self.** Visualize your inner spirit, or subtle body, ascending from your physical body. Notice that the two bodies are connected by a golden thread. This means that you can return to your physical body whenever you want to.

- **Notice how light you feel** now as your spirit body rises above your physical self.

- **Feel the effortless sensation of floating freely** yet still being connected by the golden thread.

- **As you savour this sensation,** you might choose to travel further – perhaps to another country or another time in history. You can choose to travel or you can stay where you are. Whatever you choose is right for you.

- **Now it is time for your subtle body to return** to your physical body. Visualize the two bodies gently reconnecting.

- **See yourself lying where you are now.** How did your journey evolve? Where did you go and what did you see? Take time to reflect on your astral travel.

- **Take time to think about the experience** of both the subtle and physical bodies. What can you take from this experience that will serve you well in your waking life?

- **Now it is time to bring your attention back to the room.** Ground yourself in the here and now, feeling the sensation of your body on the surface on which it lies. Gently, re-enter your waking world

CD TRACK 7

My Dream Wisdom

THIS TRACK HELPS YOU TO IDENTIFY THE GIFTS GIVEN TO YOU IN DREAM FORM, AND THE GUIDES WHO HAVE IMPARTED THAT WISDOM.

- **As you lie in your comfortable position,** think about the wise people who have visited you in your dreams. Take time to think about each one.

- **Imagine you are meeting them again.** See their faces and look at their expressions. Visualize them with you in the room now.

- **As you visualize these characters,** allow each one to speak to you — listen to their words of love and comfort. Really listen to what they tell you. Take their love and light into your heart.

- **Pause to reflect** on the kind gifts that these wise people have given to you. Remember how you have received them in your dreams.

- **Thank them for their insight.** Say the words out loud.

- **In your reflective state,** recall how your dreams have come to you to help you. Think of all the times your dreams have brought you new insights and solutions to problems. Perhaps they have helped you understand and heal relationships. Perhaps your dreams have enabled you to feel more confident and enhanced your self-esteem. The wise dream visitors may have alerted you to situations you were unaware of in your waking state. Think deeply about the gifts your dreams have brought.

- **Celebrate your inner knowledge** and thank your dreaming self for being with you all your life. From your earliest dreams in childhood to the dreams you dream now, they come in service to your health and well-being.

- **Now, as you honour your dreams** by thinking of them and seeking to understand them, ask them to continue to bring you dream wisdom.

- **Your dream world and your waking world are as one.** Embrace both with kindness and love.

- **Bring your attention back to the room.** Ground yourself in the here and now. When you are ready, roll over to one side and sit up carefully.

Index

Acknowledgements

Picture Acknowledgements
Alamy/Blend Images/Jose Luis Pelaez Inc. 18, 157; /Cultura/Frank and Helena 122; /D. Hurst 57; /Keystone Pictures USA 125; /North Wind Picture Archives 183; /Novastock/Stock Connection Blue 4 (background); /Radius Images 1, 147; /Sabena Jane Blackbird 179; /Tetra Images 189. **Corbis** 13; /Bettmann/© Salvador Dali, Fundació Gala-Salvador Dali, DACS, 2011 127; /Bloomimage 115; /Cameron Davidson 155; /Inmagine Asia 20; /Juice Images 152; /Max Power 215; /Michael Nicholson 119; /Sakamoto Photo Research Laboratory 51; /Stuart O'Sullivan 158; /Underwood & Underwood 117; /ZenShui 216. **Fotolia**/Argus 11 (background); /Irata 55; /pressmaster 120; /pst. 184; /Samantha Roche 151; /rufar 181; /Anatoly Vartanov 96. **Getty Images** 154; /Dirk Anschutz 93; /Thomas Barwick 58; /DreamPictures 53, 191; /Ingine 83; /Gary Isaacs 61; /JFB 94; /SuperStock 86, 88; /James Tse 28; /Roger Viollet 148; /Win Initiative 186. **Imagesource** 32. **Octopus Publishing Group**/Frazer Cunningham 27; /Ruth Jenkinson 2, 22, 210, 224; /Russell Sadur 9, 23, 25; /Mark Winwood 212. Photodisc 91, 214, 218. **Scala, Florence**/Digital image, The Museum of Modern Art, New York/© ADAGP, Paris and DACS, London 2011 221. **TopFoto**/Alinari Archive 31.

Managing Editor: Clare Churly
Deputy Art Director: Yasia Williams
Designer: Cobalt ID
Picture Library Manager: Jennifer Veall
Senior Production Controller: Lucy Carter